The Lost World of Floriography

Learn how in the nineteenth century hundreds of blooms were plucked to create sentimental bouquets exchanged by lovers and friends. A simple clutch of flowers could begin a clandestine love affair or declare an emotional war. A red rose is a symbol of love, but a yellow rose signifies infidelity and a white rose represents silence. A dried white rose, however, indicates something a bit more severe: death preferable to loss of innocence. Prepare yourself for a visual feast that illuminates global rituals, mythologies, and the hidden meanings nested in your favorite flowers.

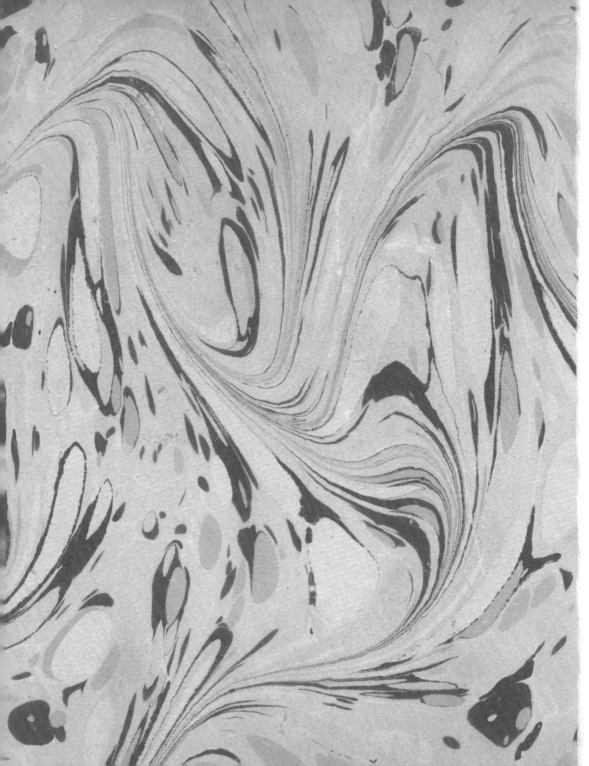

Flowers *and* Their Meanings

The Secret Language and History of Over 600 Blooms

Karen Azoulay

Foreword by Kate Bolick

Clarkson Potter / Publishers
New York

FOREWORD

A gaggle of teenage girls screaming ecstatically for the latest boy band may not seem to share much with their Victorian counterparts giggling over a floral dictionary. But like a focus on boy bands or fan fiction, the language of flowers—embedding secret messages in bouquets, according to meanings listed in special floral dictionaries—provided young women throughout the nineteenth century with a vital emotional outlet. Publishers raced to keep pace. Paging through a beautifully illustrated book, dreaming up possible floral arrangements, alone or with friends, was a fun, socially sanctioned way for girls to explore their evolving identities and the wild churn of their adolescent feelings and fantasies.

The language of flowers was so popular across North America and Europe that it made its way into the lives and works of more than a few legendary authors. As a teen, Mary Ann Evans and her girlfriends consulted a floral dictionary to give one another code names. Thereafter, she signed her letters to them using her playful *nom de bloom*, if you will: Clematis ("mental beauty"). Decades later, concerned that readers wouldn't take seriously a novel written by a woman, Mary assumed the pen name George Eliot to publish *Middlemarch*. It's hard not to wonder if her girlhood game helped inspire that decision, at least subconsciously.

Speaking of the subconscious: A teenage Sigmund Freud and a friend created their own floral language to talk about girls (known as "principles") and sexual longings. "Only in summer does the delight of the principles come into bloom. I remember a so-called rose garden, a feast of dahlias," he wrote in an 1875 letter. Twenty-five years later, Freud referred to the language of flowers in his famous *The Interpretation of Dreams.*

Oscar Wilde wore a green carnation in his buttonhole, which many people interpreted as a badge of his queerness; green was an "unnatural" color for a flower, just as the love between men was considered to be. (A century later, the hip-hop star Tyler, the Creator proudly declared his bisexuality on his 2017 album *Flower Boy.* In the song "Garden Shed," he raps, "the garden / That is where I was hidin'.") When James Joyce sat down to write *Ulysses*, he armed himself with all manner of reference materials, including a floral dictionary. No matter: Denizens of the twentieth century, consumed with their passion for progress, did their best to lock away anything associated with the past and throw away the key.

By the time artist Karen Azoulay was born, the language of flowers was nearly extinct. Everybody knew that a red rose means "love," but few people knew why, or cared. Fortunately, the metaphorical promises of blossoms and blooms transcend artificial time constraints. Azoulay's Canadian girlhood included her Moroccan aunts smearing her hands with paste from the henna plant, believed to transfer good luck. At art school, she explored a growing fascination with historical ideas that involved women, nature, decor, and mythology. In 2005, when she moved to New York City and her first roommate gave her a nineteenth-century floral dictionary of her grandmother's, the gift struck Azoulay as both intriguingly exotic and uncannily familiar.

In this gorgeous and meticulously researched new work, Azoulay shows that humans have celebrated the expressive capabilities of flowers and plants for millennia, all over the world, and will forevermore. "Think of the coded language of emoji," she writes. "Like a poetic bouquet, a chain of emojis can send a sincere message without uttering a word. It can be hard to express love, lust, and earnest declarations of praise or apology, but a combo of gimmicky symbols feels less vulnerable."

Some of my favorite books are those that take an ordinary element of everyday life and show that it's extraordinary. This is one of those books. Before reading it, I rarely thought about flowers. Now I see them everywhere, all the time—the scarlet poppies ("fantastic extravagance"), deep pink roses ("encouragement"), and purple morning glories ("affection") patterning my favorite dinner napkins; the blue hydrangea ("boaster") frilling a neighbor's sidewalk garden; my niece's daisy ("innocence") earrings. Even better, I understand now that each flower contains a story, and to learn it, all I have to do is open this book.

But this book is so much more than a floral dictionary. It is also one artist's testament to her own creative obsessions with the unexpected ways in which nature and humanity overlap. I first met Karen Azoulay in the early aughts when a mutual friend introduced us after another friend's fashion show in Manhattan's Chelsea neighborhood. I can still see us now, seated on a low, white curvilinear bench. It was summer, the air warm, and her mouth was bright with fuchsia lipstick. We immediately fell to talking, as if we were old friends already, and I felt that wonderful excitement of finding a kindred spirit, someone I could talk to forever. We could have been nine, or nineteen, in our enthusiasm and pleasure for each other. Over the years since, I've learned that like a magical witch, or a fairy godmother, she is a genius at finding beauty and meaning in what most people ignore, and makes the most ordinary moments feel special and intimate. I can't think of a better twenty-first-century ambassador for the timeless language of flowers.

Kate Bolick

INTRODUCTION

IT WAS A CROWN of orange blossoms that haloed twenty-year-old Queen Victoria on her wedding day. She loved all things floral and was very aware of the hidden meanings they projected. Fluent in the language of flowers, she knew the pale citrus blooms signified chastity, marriage, and—due to the tree's generous trait to bear fruit and flowers simultaneously—fertility. Early in their marriage, Prince Albert's grandmother gifted the young queen some myrtle, a bloom emblematic of love. Victoria had a cutting of the flower planted, and a sprig of myrtle originating from that bush has been included in every British royal wedding bouquet ever since.

One hundred forty-one years later, when twenty-year-old Diana Spencer walked down the aisle to marry Prince Charles, she held a cascading forty-two-inch-long bouquet. Following tradition, it included some of Victoria's "love myrtle." The showy floral burst featured many other botanicals, each known for a different sentiment, including ivy ("marriage"), gardenias ("transport of joy"), lily of the valley ("return of happiness"), and veronica ("fidelity"). Awkwardly tucked in behind all these white flowers, barely visible, were two canary-yellow roses. This variety of *Rosa floribunda* happened to be named after Lord Mountbatten, Prince Charles's deceased mentor and honorary grandfather. Presumably they were placed in his memory, but yellow roses are also known to signify jealousy and infidelity. Is it going too far to suspect the aggrieved Diana was expressing a complaint she could not yet dare speak aloud? This elaborate form of covert communication—broadcasting and interpreting emotions embedded in floral arrangements—is the art of floriography.

This wildly popular method of cryptologic communication captured the imaginations of many young women during the Victorian era. In the language of flowers, as it was commonly known, each botanical species was assigned a specific emotional sentiment, varying in tone from sweet (ivy geranium gallantly requested, "Your hand for the next dance?") to melodramatic (*Viburnum* declared, "I die if neglected") to downright combative (a dried white rose indicated "death preferable to loss of innocence"). A thoughtfully curated bouquet delivered a layered poetic memo for the recipient to decipher with the help of an exhaustive dictionary. Hundreds of books documenting the language of flowers were published during the nineteenth century.

Once you start looking, you will find that countless secret floral messages have been left for you to discover. In J. K. Rowling's

QUEEN VICTORIA (1819–1901) reigned over the United Kingdom from 1837 until her death in 1901.

Harry Potter and the Philosopher's Stone, the first time Professor Snape speaks to Harry, he asks, "What would I get if I added powdered root of asphodel to an infusion of wormwood?" Asphodel is a type of lily, meaning "my regrets will follow you to the grave," and wormwood represents "absence" and "bitter sorrow," translating to "I bitterly regret Lily's death."

Think of the coded language of emoji. Like a poetic bouquet, a chain of emojis can send a sincere message without uttering a word. It can be hard to express love, lust, and earnest declarations of praise or apology, but a combo of gimmicky symbols feels less vulnerable. As with floriography, this texting language was stylistically pioneered by young femmes. Since ancient times, urban youth—young women in particular—have used innovative terms that push language forward. In every generation, cries of illiteracy and vapidity belittle femme youth. In time, however, their colloquial transgressions are recognized.

Who has the need to communicate and verbally explore more than young women? I can recall talking on the phone for hours with my teenage best friend, Pam. We would meet each other at school first thing in the morning with long handwritten letters to exchange. Tightly folded into discrete shapes, these pages were filled with doodles, dreams, and quizzes about our crushes (written in secret code, of course).

Like pastel floral prints and other stereotypically feminine interests, certain language is often viewed to lack substance. Contrary to popular belief, the 1980s Valley girl *like* is not a speech filler; linguists have determined its value as a modal marker, a technique of reinforcement, and for paraphrasing. The teenage vanguard who championed an overuse of *like* are now middle aged and its use is still going strong. *Like* was not a fleeting, immature fad.

When it comes to innovative language, women and girls have a knack for finding solutions to work around linguistic or cultural barriers. Floriography allowed women to express themselves on the topics of love and romance without disrupting the prohibitive expectations of feminine etiquette. While floriography can certainly be appreciated in a frivolous way, it can also be used to craft insightful messages. Poetic expressions of tender feelings and the artful creation of handmade tokens of love are worthy of admiration and value.

The history of the language of flowers offers a unique context to investigate and question some of the larger cultural realities at play leading up to the Victorian era.

Bridal Blooms

Cultures from around the world have intuitively incorporated flowers into the celebration of matrimonial union. The Nyoro people of Uganda have a tradition of sprinkling a bride with fragrant wildflower water the morning of her wedding. Indian brides and grooms place matching garlands of flowers over each other's heads to signify happiness and prosperity.

The custom of the white bridal bouquet began in ancient Greece. Representing virginity, these bunches featured a variety of botanicals, including garlic. The ceremonial flower girl, scattering rose petals along the bridal path, can be traced to ancient Rome. Typically wearing a white dress, the child walking down the aisle symbolized the bride's loss of innocence and journey to adulthood, while the petals symbolized fertility. Later, in the Roman Empire, flower girls held a sheaf of wheat to symbolize fecundity and prosperity.

In ancient England, it was believed that a remnant of a bridal gown or bouquet would bring good luck. After a wedding ceremony, the bride was often harassed by a mob of friends and family ripping swatches of fabric from her dress or clawing at her flowers. To avoid the sometimes-brutal nature of this ritual, strategic brides began to throw their bouquets and quickly exit in the opposite direction. This tradition has lived on with the modern-day bouquet toss. It is believed that an unwed woman who catches it will be fortunate in love and life and will be next in line to marry.

ANCIENT HISTORY

TRAVELING WAY BACK in time, we see evidence of the ritualistic and sentimental connection between people and flowers since the very beginning.

THE PALEOLITHIC ERA

Neanderthal remains uncovered in northern Iraq were discovered to have been ritualistically buried with flowers. Traces of twenty-eight different botanical species were identified in the grave.

Possibly the oldest known example of a human burial decorated with plant life was found at a late Natufian gravesite in a cave at Mount Carmel in northern Israel. Impressions made in the mud lining the graves revealed evidence of Judean sage and figworts, although the significance of the plants is not known.

SIXTEENTH CENTURY BCE

Mesoamerican civilizations discovered that the morning glory flower not only had hallucinogenic properties but other useful attributes as well. Natural latex, which is the sap extracted from the Panama rubber tree, becomes brittle once it dries out. By combining latex with the juice of the morning glory flower vine, it remains pliable and tough. This process can be compared to vulcanization—a method of hardening rubber—which was not invented for another three thousand years.

The earliest known gardens in China were created more than three thousand years ago. In time, the ancient gardens developed into meditative retreats for scholars. These Chinese botanists cultivated wisterias, rhododendrons, chrysanthemums, camellias, gardenias, forsythias, lotuses, magnolias, and peonies.

THIRTEENTH CENTURY BCE

During the reign of Egyptian pharaoh Amenophis III, the tomb of the temple's chief florist was covered with depictions of his various professional tasks. The chief florist oversaw gardens and managed production crews while they created botanical arrangements. One of the most prevalent motifs in this artwork was the beloved blue lotus. Reemerging from the water every day to unfurl its sapphire petals, the bloom signified rebirth. Depicted together with stalks of the papyrus plant, the message was one of unification between Lower Egypt, represented by papyrus, and Upper Egypt, represented by the lotus.

ELEVENTH CENTURY BCE

The pharaohs of ancient Egypt valued the symbolic and spiritual nature of botanicals and were laid to rest draped with intricate flower garlands and collars. Records kept by a handful of temples reveal that Ramses III made more than a million floral offerings to the gods per year. Floral offerings were made in the hopes that the gods would bestow great fortune on the donor. Itemized inventory lists show the various types of arrangements he gave, such as fan bouquets, scented bouquets, blue flowers on strings, and floral heaps.

FIRST CENTURY BCE

Originating farther east, the "Flower Sermon" is an apocryphal story about Buddha and his disciples. When an audience of attentive students gathered to hear his teachings, the Buddha simply held up a white lotus. All but one of the students were confused as to the lesson embedded in this gesture. Sometimes referred to as "pick up flower, subtle smile," the wordless message is a pillar of Zen Buddhism, illuminating the ethereal and indescribable nature of all things.

Celebrated for her iconic, feminine wiles, Cleopatra was said to have spent the equivalent of $800 a day on perfumed floral unguents, or ointments, to rub all over her hands and arms.

FIRST CENTURY CE

In Ovid's collection of Greek mythological stories, *Metamorphoses*, women were typically associated with useful trees, like Daphne, who transformed into a laurel. Just as fanciful plumage is primarily found on male birds, it was the men of mythology, like Adonis, Hyacinth, and Narcissus, who transformed into colorful flowers. In Western culture, however, flowers were more often personified as women. We find endless examples of flowers being used to mirror the qualities of a woman and expectations that women carry themselves with the delicate purity of a spring blossom.

One of the first known serial killers in history, Locusta, is remembered for her notorious appreciation of belladonna. She was hired by the wife and adopted son of Roman emperor Claudius to murder him. After lacing the emperor's mushrooms with the deadly nightshade, Claudius's son Nero rose to power. As emperor, Nero gave Locusta a big estate and commissioned her to kill his enemies. It is rumored that she had thousands of victims. She even started a school to teach her methods to the next generation of aspiring murderers. A sadistic emperor of unsound mind, Nero was declared a public enemy by the senate. In response, he committed suicide. With her protector and patron gone, Locusta was seized and killed in retribution for her many murders.

THIRD CENTURY CE

The ancient Sanskrit sex and pleasure manual known as the Kama Sutra lists sixty-four skills that a woman of quality should hone. Several of them include delicate floristry arts, such as adorning an idol with rice and flowers, arranging beds of flowers on the ground, making artificial flowers, and crafting crests and topknots out of flowers.

Celebrated for more than fifteen hundred years, the true origin of Valentine's Day is unclear, although it is commonly associated with the Roman feast of Lupercalia. St. Valentine, a defiant priest, secretly performed marriage ceremonies in a time when Rome outlawed marriage for young soldiers. Legends tell that Valentine fell in love with his jailer's daughter. Using crushed violets growing near his cell for ink, he wrote her a note signed "your Valentine." He was executed on February 14. Although the holiday is now synonymous with red roses, it was originally violets, with their heart-shaped leaves, that represented Valentine's Day well into the twentieth century.

TWELFTH CENTURY CE

At the Games of Treviso, an Italian festival, the Castle of Love was a featured event. Unmarried women would defend the fortress—a wooden, castle-like structure made of silk curtains and carpets—while young men hailing from Treviso, Padua, and Venice came to attack it. All parties were armed with fruit, nuts, and flowers such as lilies, narcissus, violets, and roses. They would also spray each other with rose water and other perfumes. A panel of refereeing knights was tasked to declare which city won, and the women in the castle would surrender to the men of that city.

SIXTEENTH CENTURY CE

Medieval gardens prioritized growing food, medicine, and poison over the cultivation of aesthetic beauty, but symbolic modes of floral communication can be found in the culture of the era. Shakespeare crowned Ophelia with a wreath of wildflowers, mirroring the bewildered state of Ophelia's faculties. The arrangement of meadow lychnis (also known as the "fayre mayde" of France), nettles (a prickly plant), daisies (known as "day's eye" and recognized as the virgin bloom of the year), and long purples (known as dead men's hands or fingers), translated in order, could mean "The fayre mayde stung to the quick, her virgin bloom under the cold hand of death."

THIRTEENTH CENTURY CE

The Aztecs grew many flowers and decorated their homes with them. Their poetry praised marigolds, dahlias, polyanthus, and zinnia. The Aztec goddess Xochiquetzal, also known as Flower Precious Feather, was associated with fertility, beauty, and feminine sexual powers. She served as a protector of mothers and a guardian of pregnancy, childbirth, crafts, and flowers. Worshippers donned animal and flower masks in her honor.

FIFTEENTH CENTURY CE

In the fifteenth century, the heraldic Tudor rose was adopted by King Henry VII as a symbol of English unification, marking the resolution of a civil war. The rivalry between the House of Lancaster (whose insignia was a red rose) and the House of York (represented by a white rose) was known as the War of the Roses. With red outer petals and white inner petals, the Tudor rose is not a real flower but a British emblem of unity featured prominently in many British paintings, buildings, and coins.

GLOBAL BOTANY EXPEDITIONS

Plants are not part of a traditional Jewish burial or funeral. In fact, the religion has surprisingly few floral rites. Instead of bringing bouquets to a cemetery, Jewish visitors place small stones on a grave. Even the Garden of Eden is described in the book of Genesis without the mention of flowers. Any spiritual feelings or superstitious beliefs associated with the natural world could be a threat to monotheism.

Because of its connection to paganism, the Roman Catholic Church didn't trust flower symbolism and forbade ceremonial use of flora. Citizens across borders, from the Druids to the Aztecs, rebelled against restrictions and refused to give up their beloved "heathen" rites. Eventually, the Church gave in to the sensual and meaningful rituals and started to fold flower symbolism into its practices, adapting the "language" for its own religious purposes. The rose, which had symbolized love and Venus, was appropriated to represent love and the Virgin Mary.

I N THE SIXTEENTH AND seventeenth centuries, European colonists began collecting plant specimens from the Americas to send back to their countries of origin. Colonists arrived with seeds, bulbs, and cuttings, introducing some of their favorite plants from home to the new regions where they settled. Ships sailed along trade routes between the Americas, Europe, and West Africa, transferring valuable cargo, including plants, animals, goods, and diseases. Botany hunters—and the wealthy people who commissioned them—were fueled by a quest for knowledge and an insatiable hunger to possess rare and exotic specimens. This same exchange also included the displacement of African people, who were forced into agricultural slavery.

In some regards, our world of scientific understanding opened up because of global exploration. Ultimately, however, the damage caused by colonization—its negative impact on Indigenous populations and the environment—was in many ways irreparable.

Trade routes expanded by the eighteenth century, and high demand for new plants and unfamiliar species encouraged a wave of botanical exploration and experimentation, such as the first floral hybrid: a cross between a carnation and a sweet William.

In 1768, British botanist Joseph Banks joined acclaimed British explorer and cartographer James Cook on the HMS *Endeavour*, which was commissioned for an overseas expedition. The explorers visited Brazil, Tahiti, New Zealand, and Australia, and Banks returned to England with thirty thousand plant specimens. He was credited with "discovering" more than a thousand plants, eighty of which were named after him, including *Banksia serrata*, which he first encountered in the Australian bush. The plant was already known as *wiriyagan* by the Cadigal people who lived there, so while Banks did not actually discover the flower, Western credit lies with him for bringing the plant to England.

Agriculture made powerful men even more so. Plants were taken from one colonized region and transported across the ocean to be cultivated on the land of another.

Napoleon Bonaparte invaded Egypt in 1798, claiming his intent to liberate its citizens from oppression. Along with his fleet of soldiers, he brought a contingent of 167 scientists, inventors, artists, and mathematicians. The team of French researchers promptly claimed a palace in Cairo as their headquarters and began cataloging information and looting antiquities from the area. These stolen artifacts sparked great curiosity and interest in the ancient civilization in the intellectual community and the general public. This led to the creation of the field known as Egyptology.

One of the most famous artifacts uncovered during this expedition was the Rosetta Stone. As far back as 3000 BCE, ancient Egyptians recorded events with pictographic hieroglyphics, but beyond that, Europeans did not know much about the use of hieroglyphics in ancient Egyptian culture. The Rosetta Stone famously features inscriptions in ancient Greek, hieroglyphic, and Egyptian demotic scripts, which European linguists spent decades trying to interpret. In 1822, French scholar Jean-François Champollion was the first to publish a significant breakthrough. This intriguing chapter of linguistic discovery created mass enthusiasm around Middle Eastern culture and the mystery of deciphering coded or foreign language. Perhaps the secret language of flowers took off in part because it resonated with the zeitgeist of the time.

The outdated term *Orientalism* was popularized in the eighteenth and nineteenth centuries to describe the growing interest in North African, Middle Eastern, and Asian cultures. The Western craze for the language of flowers arose at a time when customs from these foreign countries were highly romanticized yet deeply misunderstood, underresearched, and undervalued. Flower dictionaries appealed to western Europeans due to the language's Turkish roots. Though there was an energetic desire for ethnic influences in European culture, there was comparatively little curiosity about the actual people, philosophies, or civilizations behind the aesthetics. Westerners often blurred distinct cultures together into a singular notion, presuming superiority in the realms of intellect and refinement.

> *Travelers, however, assure us, that the people of the East see something more in them [flowers] than mere objects of admiration. In the hands of these primitive and interesting people, they become flowers of rhetoric, and speak their feelings with far more tenderness and force than words can impart. . . . [H]ow much more refined, poetic and affecting is the mute eloquence of the Eastern lover, than those awkward and embarrassing declarations which are in use in other countries! How much easier is it to present a flower, than to make a speech!*
>
> —*E. W. Wirt*, Flora's Dictionary, *1829*

In the early 1800s in North America, explorers Lewis and Clark set off to explore the seemingly endless wilderness of the west guided by a Shoshone woman named Sacagawea. They were explicitly tasked by President Jefferson to interview Indigenous people on topics related to their agricultural knowledge and techniques. This expertise, which was traditionally preserved

Tender Recollections

For those enslaved in the antebellum American South, the opportunity to congregate and collectively grieve the loss of a life was extremely rare. With such limitations, discrete, ritualized gestures developed. The yucca was sometimes planted as a tombstone. Periwinkle flowers were so commonly scattered over the graves of enslaved African Americans that archaeologists began to discover unmarked burial sites by searching beneath patches of the perennial wildflower. The tiny buds, which signify "tender recollections," worked well as covert, meaningful markers, leading loved ones to burial sites.

Periwinkle, E. E. Gleadall, *THE BEAUTIES OF FLORA* (1834–1836); image from Biodiversity Heritage Library, courtesy of Collection of University of Wisconsin.

Lady Montagu

I**N THE EARLY 1700S,** the English aristocrat, writer, and poet Lady Mary Wortley Montagu followed her husband, the English ambassador at Constantinople, to the Ottoman Empire. Lady Montagu lived a deeply enthralled life, romanticizing Eastern culture so much that she took to wearing a turban. She became the first secular woman to write about Muslim culture. Gaining access to private spaces such as female bathhouses, she came to see how horrified her new friends were by the torturous and misogynistic corsetry that British women were forced to wear. She returned to England with valuable souvenirs: incredible stories and the technique of inoculation for smallpox.

The Middle Eastern tradition of *sélam* was among the cultural charms Lady Montagu described in correspondence. She claimed, "There is no colour, no flower, no weed, no fruit, herb, pebble, or feather, that has not a verse belonging to it; and you may quarrel, reproach, or send letters of passion, friendship, or civility, or even of news, without ever inking your fingers." This note was sent to a friend with a box containing a pearl, clove, jonquil, paper, gold wire, and pepper alongside a list translating the meaning of each object.

Lady Montagu shared her Turkish embassy letters within her social circle, a collection of which was published in 1763, the year after she died. Along with writings by traveler Aubry de La Motraye from 1727, Montagu is often cited as the source inspiration for the language of flowers. The language of *sélam* was fully described in a book about the Ottoman Empire titled *The Turkish Secretary*. Author Édouard de La Croix listed 191 objects used by those who practiced *sélam* in his dictionary, 16 of which were flowers, including "jasmin," "tubereuse," "dazy-flower,"

The Turkish have their own antiquated tradition of coded language, expressed through objects. Sélam, like the greeting "Salaam!" is also known as the Turkish love letter. A combination of objects—such as a single almond, a piece of silk, a flower, a lock of hair—would be wrapped up in a kerchief and presented as a poetic expression of emotion. Memorized rhyming schemes associated with each commonly used token allowed recipients to decipher the coded message hidden in the bundle. A Turkish publication from 1303 shows that many sélam symbols were phonologically based, reflecting the slang and vulgar colloquialisms of the era. A piece of sugar, for example, which in Turkish is called şeker, has a phonetic ring with the phrase seni midem çeker, which translates from ancient Turkish to "I crave for you."

Lady Mary Wortley Montagu,
New York Public Library Digital
Collections

LADY MARY WORTLEY MONTAGU

"paunsy-flower," and rose. Published in both French and English almost thirty years before Montagu's letters were written, some believe that her correspondents would have already been familiar with the concept of the so-called Turkish love letter. Even so, Montagu and her social circle of influence were the catalyst for the language of flowers that fascinated Europe.

Orchis Genitalis

The Clitoria *is a lovely bluish-purple orchid and one of the many flowers that bears a remarkable similarity to a vulva and clitoris. Named appropriately in 1678, the label was controversial to certain nineteenth-century botanists. In Ayurvedic medicine, the* Clitoria *is considered beneficial for women's health.*

There are also many flowers with phallic stamens. The Orchis italica *is known as "the naked-man orchid." The labellum of the flower perfectly mimics the silhouette of a human body, anatomically complete with a dangling penis. Not surprisingly, some have hoped that the flower has powers to augment virility. Orchid enthusiasts are known to hold a particular fascination for provocatively swollen, hairy, or veined features.*

CLITORIA illustration, S. Holden, *Paxton's Magazine of Botany and Register of Flowering Plants* (1834–1849); image from Biodiversity Heritage Library, courtesy of Pennsylvania Horticultural Society.

through oral traditions, was absorbed by colonists and ultimately exploited, as the contributions and knowledge of Native Americans remain mostly absent from recorded history.

Just as the potential profitability of "untouched" Australian land was apparent to botanist Joseph Banks, and Egypt was Napoleon's exploration destination, imperialism and colonization paved a tempting path to power and profit for the leaders of Western culture. Even beloved American inventor and politician Benjamin Franklin famously touted agriculture as a key to America's financial independence—though he did not explicitly mention the high cost of trading enslaved African Americans' lives and dignity for white Americans' financial "freedom."

A WIDER PERSPECTIVE

Historically, Western culture has maintained a dominating relationship over nature. All too often, history has credited European explorers with "discovering" new species of flowers. These explorers' encounters with plants on other continents are falsely presented as botanical origin stories. Flowers are often named in these explorers' honor without acknowledging a plant's indigenous roots.

The history of floral culture is typically pulled from a well of resources created from a colonial perspective. Books about the language of flowers rarely acknowledge colonialism or the fact that this massive trend took place in an era tainted by the Civil War and chattel slavery in America and the British colonies. Actively searching for forgotten histories makes our understanding of our botanical past that much richer and more interesting.

Some large institutions such as the Royal Botanic Gardens, Kew, and the New York Botanical Gardens have begun to acknowledge the direct link between the acquisition of their massive collections and colonialism. Botanical professionals who are working to improve the systemic imbalance are revising the plant histories they display and teach, sharing information—as well as intellectual and financial resources—with other educators while striving for collaboration with the countries that were unethically mined for their plants.

FLORAL AS FEMININE

The notion that flowers are feminine can be traced throughout history, but the belief gained steam toward the end of the eighteenth century. Popular gardening and flower trends often followed contemporaneous scientific advancements. When cellular structures and conservation were being studied, for example, a naturalist appreciation of wildflowers was all the rage.

The twenty-first-century focus on sustainability has amplified the importance of planting native species.

By the end of the eighteenth century, the work of Carl Linnaeus fueled an interest in the sexuality and reproduction of flowers. The Swedish botanist was known for creating a new taxonomical system, classifying plants according to their reproductive methods. The correlations Linnaeus made between plant and human sexuality were brazenly straightforward and descriptive. In *Philosophia botanica* (1751), he debated between referring to a flower's calyx as "the bedroom" or "the lips of the cunt or the foreskin."

Viewing plants through a sexual lens led to the personification of plants based on their biological attributes. This inspired sexual and romantic poetics. Titillating terms such as *hermaphroditic polygamy*, *conjugal coupling*, *eunuchs*, *genital fluid*, and *clandestine marriages* were made more arousing when hidden under the guise of plant life. Some argued that the sexualization of plant life made it possible for women to talk about the taboo subject of sex. Coded language was a safe way to tiptoe through risqué territory.

Embedded in Linnaeus's new scientific language was a hierarchy of power based on gender. Linnaeus perceived the pollen-producing stamen, for example, as masculine and more important than other floral anatomy, which he classified as passively receptive and "female." He pasted binary assumptions about human gender and sexuality onto plants, thus affirming the stifling cultural expectations and limitations placed on women.

European society's narrow understanding of botanical sexuality was often used as a metaphorical stand-in for the trappings of human sensuality and courtship. Linnaeus's binary view of masculine and feminine floral attributes perpetuated the rigid societal expectations and limitations for how all people, but especially women, were to perform their gender. It is unfortunate that the lesson gleaned from the world of plants was not one of diversity and fluidity, because there is plenty of evidence to support that view if you are looking for it.

At least 90 percent of flowering plants, including roses, tulips, and lilies, are considered bisexual. In botanical terminology, this means they contain functioning structures attributed to both masculinity and femininity. Unisexual plants, like the white mulberry or American holly, embody the sexual organs of only one gender—male or female. Polygamous plants, like the campion or forget-me-not, have both bisexual and unisexual flowers. Some plants even develop different reproductive capabilities as they morph into new stages of development.

LES FEMMES RÉVÉES—ideal beauties. Les fleurs des champs—the flowers of the fields. Created / Published C. 1851 June 9.

The Secret Language of Fans

In a time when speaking out was not always encouraged, the nineteenth century brought about several coded languages to convey romantic gestures. One of these lexicons is the language of fans. A fan held in a specific pose or flicked shut at a certain angle would broadcast clear intentions to potential suitors. Sitting in an opera box across the theater from an admirer, a lady could let "I hate you" be known by discreetly drawing the fan through her hand. Clutching it in her left hand transmitted the more encouraging "desirous of acquaintance." The era also made room for a language of parasols and a language of gloves.

Floral motifs were popular in fashion and decor; hand fan, early nineteenth century, Metropolitan Museum of Art.

Flowers were (and still are) associated with perceived "femme" qualities such as small stature, fragility in disposition and physique, and impermanence of beauty. A woman's virginity was oft compared to a delicate flower—something to be protected at all costs; the verb *deflower* is a familiar euphemism for breaking a virgin's hymen; progressing through the stages of puberty and transforming into a sexual and fertile woman was often described as "coming into full bloom." Fading in front of us, flowers represent the transience of beauty. Western culture has placed an emphasis on the fleeting youth and beauty of women who, like cut flowers, wilt and decay before our eyes.

In Victorian England and North America, women were encouraged to cultivate flower-like qualities. Etiquette books recommended that a lady not only look and smell like a flower but that she feel and think like one as well. There was a common trope in American literature at the time that if a cowboy out on the frontier came across a cabin with a rosebush outside, he knew a good woman lived there.

Frenchwomen were especially interested in feminizing themselves to be more attractive to men. Fragrance was an important element of nineteenth-century beauty and affluence. Of course, it was only women in positions of wealth and leisure who could cultivate their floral toilette. For those who could, specific fragrances were assigned to various feelings or moods.

In Europe, gardening was a suitable pastime for men, but in America it was considered a feminine activity. The broad, scientific strokes of nature and plants were associated with powerful men, but flowers and gardening belonged to women and artisans. While a male gardener labored, the perception was that a woman tended to her garden with maternal love. Whether a plant thrived or withered was a measure of her abilities to nurture.

Some botanical sentiments from this era of the language of flowers mirrored nineteenth-century gender values. Flowers with a bold and showy aesthetic that lacked fragrance were connected to low morality, whereas demure blooms with a lovely perfume were considered to exemplify the virtues of a true lady. Bright and fluffy, the hydrangea means "boaster," while the petite, aromatic white jasmine is linked to the sentiment "amiability." Another fragrant flower, lily of the valley ("return of happiness"), features small white bells praised for their humble posture, hanging down like a lady ashamed of attention and totally unaware of her beauty.

THE FLORIOGRAPHY EXPLOSION

Technological developments during the Industrial Revolution (1760–1840) transformed the realm of botany. Foreign flowers became more accessible, and home gardens flourished in tandem with a growing cultural interest in botany. The repeal of the British glass tax from the Napoleonic Wars coincided with the ability to make larger panes of glass. This made sizable greenhouses—such as the palatial Palm House at Kew Gardens—possible. Warm greenhouses allowed gardeners to grow plants from different climates, and more space meant more specimens. Each plant had unique needs, and people were dedicated to figuring out what they were.

The nineteenth century ushered in an explosion of flowers. Flower beds appeared in public parks. Affluent people built consumer-grade greenhouses. Even the urban poor could cheer up their windowsill with a box of blossoms. Floral designs appeared on every imaginable surface: wallpaper, jewelry, architecture, fans, clothing. Floral accessories were crafted out of paper, felt, shells, glass, silk, and wax with a surprising level of botanical accuracy. Though flower crowns were frowned on as an outdated pagan style, a small bloom in the hair or on a hat was considered very chic. Handheld bunches known as tussiemussies were fashionable accessories. Handkerchiefs scented with jasmine and other perfumes were commonly used to mask the foul odors of city life. Boutonnières were thought to ward off disease as well as evil, and men began wearing buttonhole and coat flowers to spruce up their attire.

During this time, the publishing world was utterly transformed by the introduction of lithography, steam-powered printing presses, and industrial paper production. Reading became a sophisticated, stylish hobby; a well-appointed library, stocked with beautifully crafted books, was considered an important feature of a respectable Georgian mansion. Literature and magazines became more accessible and middle-class families enjoyed personal libraries of their own, even if it was just a small bookcase. This paved the way for a wave of successful botanical publications.

The interest in flowers skyrocketed at a time when women led very restricted lives. They had few "appropriate" activities to explore other than writing letters (which they did in great volume). As the burgeoning genre of sentimental flower books were published, reading about flowers provided much-needed diversion from everyday life, and women's social needlepoint gatherings were replaced with floral drawing parties.

Herbs & Healing

Many herbalists following European, Native American, Indian Ayurvedic, African, and Chinese traditions believe that plants give visual clues to potential medicinal use. This theory is known as the doctrine of signatures. For example, hepatica, also known as liverwort, features a lobed leaf that resembles the human liver, leading herbalists to believe in the flower's curative benefits for that organ.

Over time, some floral remedies have proven to be effective, others not, and some quite dangerous. Many plants have been used for their curative benefits for centuries, but most herbal remedies are unregulated and have never been seriously tested for toxicity or efficacy. Some pharmaceuticals, however, do have botanical origins. The painkiller aspirin was derived from willow bark. Morphine came from the poppy. The U.S. Department of Agriculture claims that 40 percent of the medications kept behind counters in Western pharmacies were originally derived from botanicals.

Written specifically for women, the initial wave of floral books focused on poetry. Some were written as intimate letters sent from a woman in the country to the reader, with themes of morality or horticultural information sprinkled between poems. Botanical identification texts also became popular during this time, aiming to distinguish the true species cited in beloved literary texts. Many flowers' names were misleading in texts, like the Bible or the writings of Shakespeare, and these botanical identification books hoped to delineate between species.

Charmed and inspired by the romantic Turkish love letter brought to Europe by Lady Montagu, French flower dictionaries were created following a phonetic logic similar to *sélam*. Handwritten lexicons began circulating in France in the early nineteenth century—around the same time as the botanical identification guides published elsewhere in Europe—and a few small lists were published here and there. The first significant floriographic publication in the Western world was B. Delachénaye's *Abécédaire de flore ou Langage des fleurs* in 1810, which was dedicated to Napoleon's former mistress Josephine. Continuing in the tradition of the *sélam*, Delachénaye played with rhymes and word sounds. For example, he paired the plant absinthe with the word *absence*. The phonetic pairings were not, however, as obvious when these publications were translated into other languages. In the case of absinthe, many English readers were left wondering what it was about this plant—known in English as wormwood—that conjured the theme of absence. Despite translation problems such as these, the original meanings stuck.

In 1819, Louise Cortambert published *Langage des fleurs* under the pen name Charlotte de Latour. This early book was perhaps the most influential of the genre, becoming the model for all floriography books to come. Although each author made personal and artistic adjustments to the flowers included and the meanings associated with each bloom, a comprehensive and generally agreed-on lexicon of flower symbols was passed from one publication to another. For example, *The Language of Flowers* (1834) by Frederic Shoberl was an English adaptation of Latour's work with a few editorial alterations. He substituted some flowers for English blooms, such as the beloved London pride.

The template for these books was built on copying the text of previously published dictionaries. Like a game of broken telephone, a typographical or botanical error made by one author, such as the inclusion of abatina and abecedary (flowers that do not exist), was then repeated in dozens of other publications that followed. Throughout the century, new and exotic species were introduced to the marketplace, and they were added to the growing list.

AOÛT.

Tubéreuse.

Volupté.

Charlotte de Latour presents tuberose as an emblem of *volupté*, or "intense sensual pleasure"; image from Biodiversity Heritage Library, courtesy of Cornell University Library.

As the cultural appetite for the language of flowers grew, hundreds of competing flower dictionaries were published. For the most part, there was a consensus between authors on the meanings of each of the flowers typically listed. However, some flowers were commonly interpreted differently, depending on the source, leaving the potential for miscommunication. Imagine a young woman hoping to receive a bouquet and her poor suitor unknowingly presenting her with a message of "deception" and "disappointment" instead of "I am dazzled by your charms."

The trend reached England in the 1820s with Henry Phillips's *Floral Emblems*, the first substantial English publication in the genre. Because of the Napoleonic Wars and the French Revolution, the British still held a general distrust of French morality at the time, and there was a palpable rivalry between the countries. The language of flowers had to be cleansed of unwholesome French content to be more suitable for English readers. Phillips prefaced his book by explaining his avoidance of all "indelicate allusions" or "double entendres that could be offensive to modesty." His prim and proper book left little indication that the language could be applied to saucy flirtations or love affairs.

In the early nineteenth century, the French did not see romance, love, and marriage as inherently related. They were frank about sex and, in some cases, openly took lovers. English authors censored the French attitude to love, which they considered immoral. In return, the French believed that the relaxed mindset that the English held toward divorce—and the relative freedom the Brits afforded to young, single women—was immoral. Interestingly, English women tended to enjoy certain freedoms up until they married. As wives, they often found themselves to be very confined, while their French counterparts enjoyed greater social autonomy and clout after they married.

English novelist Henrietta Moriarty, who was also a moralistic botanical artist of the time, felt that the obvious sexual function of stamens and pistils had indecent implications. She believed the imagery was dangerous for young people to see. By carefully arranging the angles of each flower to hide the naughtiest bits, she purposely walked the line to make her drawings sufficiently accurate but void of any sexual allusion.

Floriography books became bestselling Christmas gifts for young women. Stunning volumes featured hand-tinted engravings, calendars, fortune-telling games, and gilded edges. For some luxe editions, the pages were even scented with violet perfume. Many were beautifully wrapped in newly developed satin bindings. The first French publications had been fancifully crafted for the upper class, but as the trend grew, books were mass-produced for middle- and working-class markets as well.

Stems of Divination

Sarah Mayo's Floral Fortune Teller *(1846) provides a game of prediction, reminiscent of the contemporary middle-school favorite,* MASH. *Participants select five individual flowers, and the "fortune-teller" reveals their destiny by translating the resulting bouquet. Each flower corresponds to a literary quote that can be read as the answer to one of Mayo's five questions. A bouquet containing a white bachelor's button, blue periwinkle, purple aster, yellow hibiscus, and red zinnia, according to Mayo's text, tells the following story:*

✎ Describing your character: White Bachelor's Button

"Sell when you can; you are not for all markets." —Shakespeare

✎ What is, or will be, the state or quality of my love? Blue Periwinkle

"A woman of a steadfast mind, Tender and deep in thy excess of love." —Wordsworth

✎ What is, or will be, my worldly fortune? Purple Aster

"Tho' poor in gear, ye're rich in love." —Burns

✎ What is the scene in which most of my life will be spent? Yellow Hibiscus

"An old deserted mansion" —Hood

✎ What is the character of my future companion? Red Zinnia

"He is but a landscape painter." —Tennyson

Flora's Interpreter

Editor of the popular magazine Godey's Lady's Book, *Sarah Josepha Hale was considered the arbiter of white middle-class taste, style, and morality. Her book* Flora's Interpreter, *was released in 1832. Hale was an abolitionist who strongly believed in education for women, but she was actually antisuffrage. She was interested in what she saw as the "secret, silent influence" that white women were able to wield in the domestic realm. Hale's is an ironic message, considering her powerful position in the culture and media landscape of the time.*

Hale is largely responsible for the invention of the American holiday of Thanksgiving as we know it today. Sensing the bubbling tension in the country, which would soon lead to the Civil War, Hale believed a national celebration might help unite those at odds. Not settling to whisper her ideas into a man's ear, she began campaigning for the feast day in 1846, petitioning every sitting president until Lincoln agreed to a national holiday in 1863. Hale used the pages of her magazine as a platform to sell her concept to the public. Set to a revisionist fantasy history of the early colonists and Indigenous peoples of America, she advocated for her vision of a long table with a big turkey at the end—as well as pumpkin pies.

Botany is one scientific discipline that did not seem to conflict with religion in the Victorian era. Charles Darwin's theory of evolution, and other cutting-edge ideas that might have been rejected by religious readers, were mostly absent from these botanical and language of flower books. An audience for Christian floral morality books developed in England and the United States, and there was even a small faction of religious practitioners who adapted the language of flowers for their purposes. It was considered a safe yet exciting genre for those whose spiritual security was threatened by scientific progress. Some performed "flower missions" to spread the gospel by simply distributing flowers to the poor and sick. They felt it was God's language that could inspire the downtrodden to rise up out of poverty and become devout Christians.

Many symbols provided in flower dictionaries were inspired by characteristics of the plant itself, such as color, shape, and odor. Folklore and myth were important influences on the metaphorical values pinned to each species as well. Yarrow, for example, earned a connection to "war" because it was used as a field poultice to heal wounds on the battlefield. Mullein became associated with health because Quaker women, who were not allowed to use cosmetics, used mullein as an illicit beauty tool to create a luminous complexion. Rubbing the foliage on their cheeks caused an allergic reaction that gave them a blushing glow.

Many books devoted chapters to the grammar of flowers and tips on how to "read" the language. For example, a marigold ("despair") conjured trouble on the mind when tucked into one's hair or hat. Worn as a corsage over the heart, however, it spoke of pangs of love.

An inverted stem was understood to negate a sentiment. For example, a red tulip ("declaration of love") screamed "declaration of hate" when presented upside down. There were complicated methodologies to communicate days of the week, months, or numbers in general as well. This information could be conveyed by meticulously lining up stems, each bearing a specific number of leaflets and berries. Using foliage to set the date for a proposed rendezvous was a chancy venture, unless you were absolutely certain which floriographic reference your correspondent relied on.

The Language and Poetry of Flowers by Mrs. C. M. Kirkland (1884) provided a list of suggested bouquets to deliver specific messages. According to Kirkland, a bunch of everlasting pea, night convolvulus, and forget-me-nots says, "Meet me to-night; do not forget." In this way, young lovers communicated under the veil of secrecy, discreetly trading stems while outwitting their chaperones.

Some of Kirkland's other floral poems read:

"Remember our rendezvous but beware of a false friend."

"I am docile and dejected, do not refuse me."

"Humility, meekness, and truth have won the love I give to thee only."

"You are fickle, indiscreet, and affected. Therefore, you are hated."

In North America, the language of flowers was connected to the upward mobility of white women writers and editors like C. M. Kirkland. Floriography books reached the United States in 1829 with both *The Garland of Flora* by Dorothea Dix and *Flora's Dictionary* by Mrs. E. W. Wirt, originally published under the simple pseudonym "A Lady."

E. W. Wirt had given handwritten copies to friends, and one of these copies fell into the hands of an interested publisher. The book was an accidental success. Out of step with the traditional list of flowers typically included in floriography books, Wirt added American flowers from the Southeast, such as *Houstonia* and goldenrod. She did her own illustrations and, in some editions, included blank pastel sheets for the reader to insert their own notes or pressings.

Flora's Dictionary also included plenty of "I" and "you" statements, which encouraged recipients of floral messages to send floral replies. An Austrian rose meaning "Thou art all that is lovely" might be reciprocated with a white catchfly: "I fall into the trap laid for me." In a different scenario, some purple pansies meaning "You occupy my thoughts" could inspire a gift of spiderwort: "I esteem, but do not love you."

With the proliferation of floriography and floral poetry books in the nineteenth century, botany was perceived as a sophisticated, genteel hobby. Preserving flowers in the pages of an album to create an herbarium was a popular hobby and an innocent way to appreciate God's creations. The pressed flowers could be examined for botanical study or kept as a diaristic log of natural encounters. Many historical figures of the era, such as Harriet Beecher Stowe, Emily Dickinson, and Florence Nightingale, built impressive collections of their own.

Collaborative friendship albums—a popular type of scrapbook—were brimming with botanical themes. This opportunity to creatively relish social pursuits was mostly reserved for white women, but there are a few intact African American friendship albums in existence. These young women, born to free parents in the middle class, likely received albums as gifts for a special occasion. Mary Ann Dickerson of Philadelphia was eleven years old when she started her friendship album in 1833. Her pages were

NARCISSUS, SCARLET, GERANIUM, MARIGOLD.

This hand-tinted illustration of narcissus, scarlet geranium, and marigold translates to "Your self-love and stupidity excite my pity"; illustration by Henrietta Dumont (1851), image from Biodiversity Heritage Library, courtesy of Cornell University Library.

African Flowers

Many of the most popular and trusted tomes on the subject of flowers promise readers that Sub-Saharan Africa does not have a flower culture. This perception has been reinforced by historians and anthropologists as a way of differentiating African culture from that of Eurasia. The idea originated from a hypothesis that the continent's arid, bloomless landscapes and poor economies could not support a wide-reaching flower culture and that Africans only value flowers for nutrition and medicine. How could this sweeping generalization possibly be true? The massive continent features cultural as well as geographic diversity—South Africa alone is home to twenty-two thousand native species of flora.

Ugandan prince, anthropologist, and writer Dr. Akiki Nyabongo was passionate about correcting this misconception. In the kingdom of Bunyoro, from which he hailed, flowers were used not only for decoration and perfume but also as cultural metaphors. In 1937, Nyabongo collected three hundred specimens that were known to hold symbolic meaning. The following year, he published an essay, "Ebito or Flower Language," detailing the ancient traditions. Messages of love, hate, approval, and disapproval could be communicated through gifts of flowers, leaves, twigs, and stones. For example, one variety of the white-blooming Asparagus africanus *is said to communicate "You are the puberulus that grows at the side of the road and grasps the barkcloth of every passerby, and I will grasp at your love."*

filled with floral watercolors and poetic passages riffing on the symbols found in the language of flowers. It was a way that these young African American women could collaboratively document their personal feelings and explore values such as virtue, innocence, and chastity.

For a topic that was so often trivialized as a woman's hobby, many American floriography books were penned by noteworthy women of historical consequence. Editor Sarah Josepha Hale held a dominant position in culture and media. Nurse Dorothea Dix was an advocate for the mentally ill and established the first generation of asylums in the United States. Writer and editor C. M. Kirkland received many accolades for her books about frontier life. The various political perspectives and beliefs that these women held exemplified the tension between progress and reaction in the nineteenth century.

By the 1830s, flower dictionaries were an established trend in France, England, and the United States. Although it is often considered the Victorian language of flowers, the queen's reign did not begin until 1837. Queen Victoria and Prince Albert were a modern royal couple, interested in the au courant garden styles and using landscape design as a tool to express power, wealth, and dominance over nature. The Crystal Palace Exhibition, organized by Albert in 1851, was the first event to expose the English public to exotic plants and flowers. Guests to the midcentury event included Charles Darwin, Charlotte Brontë, and Lewis Carroll. The once-exclusive Kew Gardens expanded in size, and working-class people were encouraged to visit and enjoy.

Botany was considered the only acceptable realm of science for a woman to study, which resulted in a surge of women entering the field. Many jumped at the opportunity to make a name for themselves and collected vast herbariums, leading to a great age in botany and botanical illustration. Even though they were rarely accepted into the professional realm, a generation of women drew exquisite renderings of plants that not only moved science forward but also helped define the century.

Women pursuing this discipline were often the daughters or wives of botanists or botanical illustrators. If they were lucky enough to have patriarchal support, they could receive training. Women were often hired because they provided significantly cheaper labor, although many of them were never acknowledged for their important work. Often, their husbands were given credit. Other times, women were simply published anonymously and then forgotten. Though the prominence of botanical art was driven mostly by enthusiastic women, female botanical artists worked away in obscurity and were mostly ignored or trivialized by critics.

Self-denigration is all over the pages of books written by Victorian women. They apologize for the egotism of having written a book in the first place. Even Anne Pratt, one of the most successful female botanical artists of her time, prefaces *Flowers and Their Associations* (1840) with a plea that she "hopes these pages may not be unacceptable." In the preface to *Flora's Dictionary*, E. W. Wirt practically trips over herself to apologize: "This little play of fancy . . . has not the vanity to attach any serious consequence to it."

Les fleurs animées by J. J. Grandville was an 1847 parody of the language of flowers craze, featuring illustrations of ladies costumed to embody specific flowers in a variety of social scenarios, such as a rosebud queen presiding, thorny scepter in hand, over her loyal beetle subjects. One chapter heading reads, "Where we show that the language of flowers may cause a man to lose the tip of his nose."

Another subset of floriography books focused on botanical fortune-telling. People have always searched for reassuring predictions to calm the agony of life's uncertainty, especially when it comes to matters of the heart. Whether it is through tarot cards, horoscopes, or Magic 8-Balls, we all want answers! Not surprisingly, floral fortune-telling games were very popular with young women throughout the nineteenth century. One that is still practiced today is the classic daisy game, plucking petals to the alternating refrain "He loves me, he loves me not."

Despite the prudery of the era, change was in the air. Shortly after attending the first women's rights convention in Seneca Falls, New York, in 1848, Amelia Jenks Bloomer was inspired to get involved in the movement. Believing that the best way for a woman to share her political views was through the written word (rather than public speaking, which was commonly believed to be inappropriate for women), she started a newspaper. Considered by many to be the first American woman-owned and woman-operated publication, *The Lily* focused on issues such as temperance, women's rights, suffrage, and dress reform. Many of the contributors were influential women she had met at the convention, such as Susan B. Anthony, and Elizabeth Cady Stanton, who wrote under the pen name "Sunflower."

In the middle of the nineteenth century, radical women like Stanton, Anthony, and Bloomer began testing out dress reform. The Freedom Dress, also known as the Turkish Dress, consisted of a short dress over ballooned trousers, quite similar to the *shalwar kameez* of Central and South Asia. Bloomer promoted this new way of dressing in *The Lily*, which led to the scandalous garment's new name: "bloomers."

J. J. Grandville's *LES FLEURS ANIMÉES* (1847) is an illustrated parody of the ubiquitous publishing trend; image from Biodiversity Heritage Library, courtesy of the Research Library, Getty Research Institute.

Victorian Wo

Botanical

OF all hues, Celestial, Roseate, and gold
And glittering in elegant Splendour, behold
The LILIES, a race to whom Nature has lent
All her Loveliest charms, of Form, Colour, and Scent
With so many pleasing allurements endowed
And by so many light-winged Votaries wooed.
That through all the wide circle of Flora's domain
Where the Lover, & the Graces so constantly reign
What Tribe can be found, so varied, so fair,
Whose forms are so Noble, whose Painting so fair

TIGER LILIES illustrated by
Priscilla Susan Bury from *A Selection
of Hexandrian Plants, Belonging to
the Natural Orders Amaryllidae and
Liliacae* (1831–1834); image from
Biodiversity Heritage Library, courtesy
of Missouri Botanical Garden.

men & Illustration

JANE WELLS WEBB LOUDON WROTE and illustrated pop garden manuals such as *Instructions in Gardening for Ladies* (1840) and *The Ladies' Flower-Garden of Ornamental Bulbous Plants* (1841). One of her earliest publications was a science fiction novel titled *The Mummy!* An early example of the genre, Loudon's story takes place in 2126 and is filled with inventive predictions such as espresso machines, air conditioners, an early internet, and women wearing trousers.

Despite her undeniable talent, **Augusta Innes Withers** was rejected by the Royal Botanic Gardens, Kew, from being a botanical painter simply because she was a woman. Mrs. Withers (as she signed all her work) taught drawing to Queen Adelaide, and in later years, Queen Victoria purchased one of her sketchbooks and appointed her Flower and Fruit Painter in Ordinary. Despite these honors, she was penniless. Withers died in obscurity in a lunatic asylum in London.

Botanist and illustrator **Priscilla Susan Bury**'s work was reviewed as one of the best color-plate collections of its time, gaining a subscriber base that included John James Audubon. The humble preface to her 1831 book, *A Selection of Hexandrian Plants*, states that she "relies on the indulgence and courtesy of those more able and learned promoters, or generous admirers of botanical pursuits, who may be induced to patronize the feeble attempts of an Amateur."

A hand-colored engraving made from an Augusta Innes Withers illustration (1827–1828); image from Wikimedia Commons, courtesy of The Royal Horticultural Society Diary.

Like the language of flowers, this fashion was inspired by Turkish culture. Adornments with an Eastern influence, such as tassels; crescent-shaped brooches; rich, colorful embroidery; and even turbans, were coveted accessories. This happened just as the United Kingdom, France, and Sardinia teamed up to protect the Ottoman Empire from Russia. The curiosity about Turkish culture was perhaps due to public sentiment toward their ally of the moment, although there is a larger story when we think about Eastern influence in Europe.

In 1853, Japan, which had been sealed off from European contact for more than two hundred years, opened itself up for trade. Sudden access to imported ceramics, textiles, fans, and artwork from Japan became all the rage. After centuries of intense trade and power play via the East India Trading Company, the British Crown took control of India in 1858. In time, Queen Victoria gave herself the title Empress of India. Toward the end of the century, bohemian women of the aesthetic movement started to wear flowing tea gowns inspired by kimonos, and "Orientalist" influences can be seen in Western art of all disciplines.

The passion for floriography began to decline for the French just as their interest in astrology, demonology, phrenology, and the predictions of Nostradamus gained momentum. In time, interest tapered in England and North America, too. The fad's burnout coincided with some major cultural changes. Charles Darwin's *On the Origin of Species* was published in 1859, the telephone was invented in 1876, and by the 1890s the fight for women's rights was in full swing.

In the late nineteenth century, suffragists around the globe selected flowers as their emblems. New Zealanders wore camellias to show support for the cause, and in 1893 they became the first country to fully ratify women's right to vote. The suffragists in England chose violets. When Susan B. Anthony and Elizabeth Cady Stanton campaigned in Kansas, they adopted the state flower and wore sunflower pins. During a clincher fight in Tennessee, the suffragists wore yellow roses, and those opposed wore red roses. To this day, the gravestone of Susan B. Anthony is famously covered with "I Voted" stickers and bunches of sunflowers.

British suffragettes used the public assumption of female gentility to their advantage as a way to protect themselves from police brutality at their rallies and events. The activists decorated venues with strategically placed floral arrangements laden with lengths of barbed wire. Donning their big hats and otherwise cumbersome lady costumes of the day, women who had secretly trained in jujitsu stationed themselves near the flowers. If a police officer or other aggressive man came charging toward a speaker, she would grab him and slam him into the sharply spiked bouquet.

By the 1880s, the language of flowers trend had waned, *Language of Flowers* by Kate Greenaway (1884); image from Biodiversity Heritage Library, courtesy of Smithsonian Libraries.

As women found new freedoms and ventured into new domains, depictions of the more conservative floral feminine seemed to rise. Painters like John Singer Sargent and James Abbott McNeill Whistler painted languishing women as if they were supple flowers themselves. This glamorous imagery could be seen as a dreamy but stern reminder of a woman's place as a delicate creature.

The romantic aesthetic declined slowly in the United States and England, but more abruptly in France. By the end of the century, culture became more urban focused, and women's enthusiasm for botany as a hobby declined.

Kate Greenaway's 1884 book, *The Language of Flowers*, marked the end of the sentimental flower trend. Her illustrations include garden blooms in cute woven baskets, but they are outnumbered by images of dancing cherubs, ladies sunning themselves in pastel gowns, weeping children, and even a puppy with a pink ribbon leash. The look and tone of this dictionary was a far cry from where the genre began, with its handsome volumes, featuring botanically accurate etchings of flowers, hand tinted in rich jewel tones. Despite these differences, as the last notable publication, it somehow secured itself as a hallmark, with continued popularity and many editions printed over the years.

European artists were inspired by the Japanese art they were exposed to in the late nineteenth century. *A COLLECTION OF LIVELY SKETCHES [OF FLOWERS AND INSECTS] OF THE MING DYNASTY,* Ōoka Shunboku, 1812, Metropolitan Museum of Art.

ROOTS

Why are people so drawn to these customs from another time? The Victorian era is an accessible link between ancient and modern times. It was a period of tremendous growth and transformation. My hometown, Toronto, was built up during the nineteenth century. There is only one building still standing that predates 1800—and only by six years. My own Jewish ancestors spent the nineteenth century in diverse locations. Half were scattered across Morocco (a few even lived in caves) and the other half in cities and shtetls in Belarus and Austria. It's not likely any of them knew of floriography, with the exception of those in Austria, as there were German-language flower dictionaries.

I grew up surrounded by rituals and superstitions from Morocco, my father's land of origin. I have fond memories of my palms being smeared with henna to the sound of my aunts' ululations. Made from the symbolically potent, flowering plant Egyptian privet, henna paste is believed to transfer good luck and protection as the temporary dye seeps into the skin. Perhaps this is where my fascination with sentimental taxonomies began.

Women & Flowers

THERE ARE MANY EXAMPLES OF WOMEN from the nineteenth and early twentieth centuries who used botanical knowledge—accessible to them through their mothers, grandmothers, and larger community—to help them become trailblazers.

SUSAN LA FLESCHE PICOTTE

La Flesche Picotte combined healing practices from her Omaha heritage with Western medicine. Graduating from medical school in 1889, she was the first Native American woman to become a licensed physician.

HARRIET TUBMAN

Revered as a heroic abolitionist, Tubman was both a naturalist and herbalist. During her thirteen missions to help free seventy enslaved people through the Underground Railroad, she used botanical knowledge to read the landscape, quiet babies, find food, relieve pain, and clean wounds. Herbal practices were strictly outlawed on plantations in fear that this knowledge would empower the enslaved people with the ability to poison their tormentors. This wisdom had been covertly passed down by Tubman's grandmother.

AKIKO YOSANO

Born in 1878 in Osaka, Japan, Akiko Yosano was a celebrated feminist writer who was known for her use of floral imagery. Her first book, *Tangled Hair*, created quite a sensation with its direct portrayal of female sexuality. The publication, written in the ancient form of tanka poetry, notoriously broke barriers as the first of its kind to mention breasts. Yosano's work was revolutionary for its public depiction of sexually liberated women, which greatly contrasted the expected conventions that a lady should be modest and demure. In 1910, Yosano coauthored the first Japanese publication on the language of flowers, *Hana*.

EDITH WHARTON

Edith Wharton is known to have played with floriographic symbols in her novels, most notably in *The Age of Innocence.* Published in 1920, the story relies heavily on floral symbolism, with the character Newland Archer using bouquets to communicate his feelings for the women in his life. Wharton herself bonded with a lover, Morton Fullerton, exchanging botanical mementos in their written correspondence—even pressing the thin stem of a flower into her diary to (it has been speculated) mark the day when they consummated their relationship.

GERTRUDE STEIN

As culture shifted, flowers were sometimes trivialized. This ambivalent tone is perfectly captured in Gertrude Stein's iconic poem "Sacred Emily:" "Rose is a rose is a rose is a rose." Since there is no absolute, original source of signification for a specific flower, and because there are so many contradictory meanings, perhaps it symbolizes nothing. But no. Flowers continued to maintain an important role in intimate communications as well as shaping larger cultural movements.

A page from Edith Wharton's diary. Courtesy of Lilly Library, Indiana University, Bloomington, Indiana.

I have always been inspired by cultural practices that link emotional meaning with natural elements.

Comb through dusty old volumes in archives and libraries and there is always a special thrill coming across the odd botanical memento preserved between the pages. I've been delighted by treasures like a delicately pressed sprig of wildflowers picked from the gravesite of Willa Cather and her partner, Edith Lewis, or a leaf tucked into a three-hundred-year-old Bible. Beautiful herbariums from the nineteenth century contain floral specimens that have been carefully stitched onto the paper or placed with thin ribbons of paper tape. Each flower is typically labeled with either scientific or personal information, depending on the creator's purpose. Carefully turn the pages of these delicate albums—it is astounding to see how perfectly preserved these blooms remain after two hundred years.

Inspired by these impressive collections, I decided to begin my own flower diary. In an attempt to raise my spirits from a bout of depression, I set forth to snag blossoms (when appropriate) to commemorate significant events for one calendar year. I pressed and archived each botanical memento with a note to connect it to an event. There were many memorable days that year: weddings, funerals, a trip to Spain, protests, simple walks in my neighborhood, and my fortieth birthday. Aside from having many of the benefits that journaling provides, it was helpful to be on the lookout for little bursts of colorful positivity. I always had flowers on my mind. Even though this practice was not directly connected to floriographic symbols, it strengthened my personal connection to flowers and what they mean to me.

Sometimes the significance of a particular plant might be uniquely intimate or tied to a special memory. I got bunches of eucalyptus from the farmers' market around the time my husband and I got married, so I've thought of it as our signature foliage. One of our sweetest afternoons was spent lying in the grass, looking up at the branches of a magnolia. I've since claimed the magnolia tree as "our tree."

My husband, George, knows how to give flowers. He once gave me some extraordinary wine-red peonies and pink lupines from Seattle's Pike Place Market. He carried them on his cross-country flight home to Brooklyn. Over the years, I have been the recipient of many sad, wilting, last-minute corner-store bouquets from otherwise well-meaning sweethearts. Flowers do not need to be expensive or rare, but they must be alive! When a half-gone bouquet is the only option, I suggest tearing it apart, presenting the few lively flowers, and tossing the rest . . . or getting chocolate instead.

A friend of my husband's family was given a copy of the flower dictionary I self-published in 2015, and we began corresponding through the mail. In our handwritten letters, we discussed various topics, but covertly, and without ever acknowledging it, we would load our letters with additional messages. Coded memos were shared via carefully selected combinations of floral postal stamps or collaged postcards. During a visit to San Francisco, I was invited to finally meet him in person. His apartment was a fantastical art installation featuring a precariously hung chandelier of hot-glued Barbie dolls and a fireplace mantel framed with a rainbow arch of taped pages, torn from vintage gay nudie magazines. He prepared a special lunch with edible flowers and herbs listed in my dictionary. Each course was presented with a dramatic flair. The gray broth of his "Suspicion Soup!" had a curious flavor, but the full experience was one of the loveliest gifts I have ever received.

Eating flowers has been a recurring motif in my artwork. It's a way to explore the theme of vulnerability. For one particular video shoot, I filled a few buckets with flowers sourced from organic farms as well as flower shops and grocery stores. The symbolism attributed to each flower was most significant to me and I envisioned the piece as a botanical poem of sorts where I would consume some of the flowers on camera. I was having fun playing with the different flowers, folding pansies between my teeth or messily chomping down on a marigold. Next was an elegant calla lily. I took a bite and grimaced as I instantly realized— the flower is poisonous! While I rinsed my burning mouth out with water, my friend Rachel looked it up on her phone, finding websites listing calla lilies as not merely poisonous but fatally so! The flower, it turns out, contains insoluble microscopic crystals that stab at the tongue, gums, and throat tissue, causing pain and swelling. I decided I was probably going to be fine but said to her, "In the unlikely chance that I die, please honor my wishes for everyone to know that I died eating a poisonous flower for my art."

Botanical mementos I collected from weddings, funerals, a trip to Spain, protests, simple walks in my neighborhood, and my fortieth birthday, all preserved in an archival laminate.

BABY'S BREATH

SOMEHOW OUR collective imagination has confined the floral aesthetic of the Victorian era to one much lacier and more pastel hued than it actually was. Rich colors were preferred, and tree branches, clusters of fruit, and assorted foliage were common elements of dramatic floral arrangements. A centerpiece incorporating delicate, seasonal stems such as violets, forget-me-nots, and fuchsia typically lasted for only one night. It was understood to be an honor to share the fleeting luxury of a floral display with your dinner hosts. These days, longevity is considered one of the most important attributes for a cut flower. Tall and sturdy blooms, shipped in from around the globe, are sought after and readily available. The same vase of contemporary blooms could add a splash of color to a week's worth of dinner parties if you were so inclined.

Just as fashions shift today, floral trends constantly renewed themselves during the nineteenth century—about every twenty years or so. Chrysanthemums, which were an expensive and fussy hothouse species, were once coveted by the wealthy. Now that they are one of the most affordable flowers, they no longer carry the same cachet.

So, why is baby's breath missing from this dictionary? The ubiquitous spray of hardy white blooms was simply not a thing in the Victorian era. Known as soapwort at the time, *Gypsophila* gained the common name baby's breath toward the end of the century, which is around the same time that it became available as a garden plant. It was not used as a filler in bouquets, and it certainly was not included in the language of flower dictionaries.

The internet is clogged with conflicting lists of flower symbolism, especially those with supposed Victorian floral meanings. So much of the language of flowers is romanticized; enthusiasts have crammed every flower into the phenomenon, giving blooms all sorts of different meanings. Florists often edit out all negative associations from the nineteenth century, replacing them with only the most cheerful (and merchandisable) symbols.

Many of our most popular flowers today were not included in Victorian-era flower dictionaries. Some newer blooms, like those listed on the following page, seem to have developed symbolism that is gaining acceptance. As the tradition continues to evolve, meanings are attributed for a variety of reasons.

Alstroemeria

Devotion; Powerful friendship
Also known as **Peruvian Lily**.

Baby's Breath

Everlasting love; Purity
Also known as **Soapwort, Gypsophila**.

Catnip

Feline magic; Intoxication;
To capture someone's heart

Echinacea

Spiritual warrior;
Strength and health

Floss Flower

Politeness
Also known as **Ageratum, Blue Mink**.

Freesia

Lasting Friendship; Innocence

Liatris

Bliss; Happiness; Joy
Also known as **Gayfeather, Purple Poker**.

Lisianthus

Appreciation

Orange Rose

Thank you; Congratulations; Enthusiasm

Peach Rose

Gratitude; Sincerity

Purple Rose

Enchantment; Majesty

Sea Holly

Attraction; Independence

Stargazer Lily

Wealth and prosperity

Waxflower

Lasting love and success

Something to keep in mind is that not all flowers are available at the same time. While you can rest assured that most any flower shop will have roses, carnations, and lilies available in a variety of colors, a lovely branch of cherry blossoms is an unlikely offering at any time other than the spring.

HOW TO USE
A FLOWER DICTIONARY

THERE ARE MANY MEANINGFUL ways to use a flower dictionary. The language of flowers is not necessarily straightforward, but it can inspire readers to get creative with natural materials to convey emotions and engage with others.

Of course, the classic way to use floriography is to express yourself through a bouquet. When gifting a symbolic bunch, a simple note detailing the flowers alongside their symbols (or a companion dictionary) is always well received. It's the extra touch that makes the gift more meaningful. Another benefit is that a card will be a lasting reminder of the lovely blooms long after they have wilted away.

To compose an elaborate arrangement containing a poignant message, start with a list. The Mood Index on page 244 presents a selection of flowers organized by themes, such as flirtation, love, and apologies. You could also go directly to the florist and take note of what they have available that day. Look up their associated sentiments. Compile a list of your contenders and proceed from there. Let the florist, who might appreciate the creative challenge, in on it. This is especially important if you are ordering a bouquet online or over the phone to be delivered. Confirm with the florist that nothing will be added other than the specific flowers requested. Adding a few lovely stems of maidenhair fern ("discretion") to balance out an arrangement meant to celebrate the birth of a child might seem a bit odd.

Although my social circle knows of my passion for this topic, I have warned many dears in my life that if I give them flowers, I am not using floriography unless I tell them I am! It can be a daunting challenge to enter a florist's shop full of vibrant blooms and realize they all signify something utterly inappropriate for the circumstance of your bouquet. While a bunch of double violets ("reciprocal friendship") is a perfect sentiment for your best friend's birthday, you'll need to steer clear of sweet *Scabiosa* ("widowhood") for her wedding shower.

The language of flowers can also be used to compose coded messages in poetry, visual art, or other creative concoctions. Another alternative to an arrangement in a vase is a floral drink or edible treat. Loose petals or full blooms make a lovely garnish for a salad or cake (make sure your choices have been grown to be edible!). Perhaps meditating on the symbolism of "energy in adversity" while sipping on a hot mug of chamomile tea can help you soldier through a challenging situation.

ABOUT THIS DICTIONARY

THE FLORAL SYMBOLS COMPILED in this dictionary have been gathered from historically significant nineteenth-century publications. When a flower appears in various sources with conflicting definitions, I made a considered editorial decision to present the symbolism I determined to be the most relevant. To avoid confusion, I swapped some of the British floral common names for their American counterparts. The anecdotes listed alongside each entry touch on a variety of subjects, including superstition, mythology, old wives' tales, global history, and botanical medicine, which has been practiced by people from every region of the world. The herbal approaches described here range from well-established remedies to the obviously absurd. Between these two polarities exist many potent preparations. Many folk healing traditions have been overlooked or denigrated, and others have caused serious harm. Hopefully in time, they will be properly studied for efficacy and safety. My interest here is in exploring the emotional intentions and creative ingenuity that people continue to bring to flowers.

In the nineteenth century, comparisons between women and flowers were used to control and limit how the former expressed themselves in society. Many female artists, writers, scientists, and amateur enthusiasts mined the richness of botany and found clever ways around these restrictions, developing new ways to communicate. Recorded history focuses on power-hungry war heroes and explorers, but what about the often overlooked, intimate details of everyday life, such as the rituals of romantic courtship or how friendship is expressed? The ongoing work of nurturing, healing, teaching, and developing language is rooted in the act of caring and, yes, sometimes sentimentality. Femme culture is a powerful and important part of our collective history. I'm playing with these values by collaging my photographic images alongside botanical illustrations from the 1800s. The silver hands, mouths, and eyes reference different forms of expression. A blossom on the tip of the tongue is a lighthearted way to "say it with flowers."

To identify with flowers, we need not limit ourselves to the polite modesty of petite, pale blooms with heads bowed in shame. We must embrace complexity, holding both the delicate beauty of a carmine hibiscus and the prickly, misanthropic thorns of the fuller's teasel at once. Let's emulate the inspired burst of a stalk of angelica and mirror the bright wit of the ragged-robin, the audacity of the larch, the mature charms of the cattleya orchid, and the legendary strength of a bunch of yellow fennel.

Is there a flower that best describes how you feel about someone special in your life? Why not let them know?

Dhalia. Iris. Tulipe. Lilas. Œillet. Hortensia. Anémone. Muguet. Pivoine. Jasmin. Rose. Chèvrefeuille.

LES FLEURS, The New York Public Library Digital Collections.

ACACIA

ACANTHUS

ADONIS

A

Acacia

FRIENDSHIP

Also known as **Mimosa.** A good friend to the Indigenous people of Australia, the flowering acacia tree has been a trusted source of food, medicine, waterproofing, and decoration for tens of thousands of years. Tannins extracted from the bark are used in leather production, and the wood can be carved into useful tools such as boomerangs and spears. The ancient Egyptian medicinal text the Ebers Papyrus suggests using a paste of dates, honey, and acacia smeared onto wool and inserted vaginally as a method of birth control. The puffy yellow blooms are better known in Australia as **golden wattle**. Renowned as the national flower, Aussies celebrate Wattle Day annually on the first of September.

Rose Acacia
Elegance

Yellow Acacia
Secret love

Acanthus

THE ARTS

The unique silhouette of the acanthus leaf has long been a source of visual inspiration. The stone capitals atop Corinthian columns were ornamented with stylized acanthus leaves, and a luxurious pattern of swirled, interlocking acanthus leaves was the most iconic of textile designer William Morris's Victorian-era creations.

Adonis

SORROWFUL REMEMBRANCE

Also known as **Red Morocco, Blood Drops, Pheasant's Eye**. The Adonis flower is said to have grown from the grave of the mythological figure of the same name. Adonis, a Greek shepherd, was one of the goddess Aphrodite's lovers. Fueled by jealousy, Ares, the god of war, orchestrated a vicious boar attack to kill Adonis. Beautiful red blooms emerged where Aphrodite's tears mingled with her lover's blood. As consolation, the goddess was promised that the Adonis flower would return every year.

Agrimony

THANKFULNESS

A long stalk of bright yellow blooms, agrimony has been used for many ancient medicinal purposes. The dried herb has been used to alleviate a wide variety of symptoms, including mild diarrhea and warts. The Anglo-Saxons boiled agrimony with milk; this concoction was believed to help with erectile dysfunction.

Almond Blossom

HOPE

Often the first hint of spring, early almond blooms appear on bare boughs. In the biblical tale of Aaron's rod, God commands each of the twelve tribes of Israelites to present a staff as a means of determining priestly responsibilities. When Aaron presents his staff to represent his tribe, his stick suddenly blossoms with flowers and ripe almonds. Aaron is called on to be high priest and for those of the tribe of Levi to carry certain spiritual rights and responsibilities in the temple.

Almond
Indiscretion

Aloe

GRIEF; RELIGIOUS SUPERSTITION

Aloe is a well-known soothing ointment for painful burns, but it also has historical associations with assuring safety and peace against agonizing situations. Muslims and Jews in Cairo used to hang aloe over their doorways for protection from evil.

AMARANTH

ALOE

FLOWERS AND THEIR MEANINGS \

AGRIMONY

ALYSSUM

AMARYLLIS

ALMOND BLOSSOM

Alyssum

TRANQUILITY

Alyssum grows in cloud-like clusters composed of hundreds of tiny flowers. Translated as "without madness," the ancient Greeks thought that if consumed, alyssum could calm anger. It was also used to treat bites from rabid animals.

Sweet Alyssum
Worth beyond beauty

Amaranth

IMMORTALITY

Also known as **Love Lies Bleeding, Tassel Flower**. Purple amaranth has been a dietary staple in many Indigenous cuisines of Central America from as far back as 4000 BCE. At one point, the nutritious flower was almost as commonly dispersed as corn. It is known in Nahuatl as *huautli,* which means "the smallest giver of life." The tiny kernels can be popped like popcorn. A Mexican sweet named *alegría* (the Spanish word for happiness) is made by mixing the puffed amaranth with honey.

Globe Amaranth
Unchangeable

Amaryllis

PRIDE

Also known as **Naked Lady**. The bold amaryllis blooms with colorful trumpet-shaped flowers on a bare stalk and sparkles in candlelight. Naturally appearing in the spring and summer, the amaryllis is often forced to bloom in the winter season, as the flower has become a popular Christmas gift.

Amethyst

ADMIRATION

The amethyst flower shares its striking coloring (and name) with a violet-hued strain of quartz. According to the practice of crystal healing, amethyst is regarded as extremely powerful in balancing emotional highs and lows. The leaves of the amethyst flower are used as a folk medicine by the Ingano people of Colombia; chewed-up leaves are packed around molars exhibiting dental decay in order to relieve pain.

Anemone

FORSAKEN

Translated from Greek as "the wind's daughter," the anemone tends to grow on elevated land where it is exposed to strong gales. In Egypt, anemones were viewed as a symbol of sickness due to the belief that if you inhaled air tainted by these flowers, you would fall ill.

Field Anemone
Sickness

Angelica

INSPIRATION

Also known as **Wild Celery**. In seventeenth-century England, a monk who claimed that the archangel Michael appeared to him insisted that this flowering plant was a cure for the plague. Believing that this antidote protected a whole town, the plant was named in the angel's honor.

ANGELICA

ANEMONE

FLOWERS AND THEIR MEANINGS \

AMETHYST

*ANGEL'S
TRUMPET*

APPLE BLOSSOM

Angel's Trumpet

FAME

Shamans from Indigenous communities across the northern Peruvian Andes have been known to use angel's trumpet for ritualistic purposes and therapeutic divination. Victorian ladies would drop a tiny dose of the pollen into their tea for a hallucinogenic sensation. Scientific journals have since reported, however, that the effects of this toxic flower are violently unpleasant and may include psychosis and temporary insanity. In one extreme example, after drinking one cup of the tea, a young man cut off his own penis and tongue.

Apple Blossom

PREFERENCE

John Chapman, famously known as Johnny Appleseed, crossed great distances to spread this fruit tree across America. He planted seeds in fenced-in nurseries, left the trees to the locals, and would periodically return to check in on them. Apple trees planted from seed, however, do not produce edible fruit. Chapman's express purpose was fermentation. In rural places in the early nineteenth century, alcoholic apple cider was more important than wine, coffee, or any other beverage, including water. During the later years of Prohibition, the FBI chopped down these sour apple trees that had been used to make booze.

Apple
Temptation

Crabapple Blossom
Ill nature

Arborvitae

UNCHANGING FRIENDSHIP

Also known as **Canoe Tree, Western Red Cedar.** The Indigenous Klallam people of the Pacific Northwest use the arborvitae tree to build canoes. The Coast Salish people of this region refer to the tree as "long life maker." The Latin name translates to "tree of life."

Arum

ARDOR

Also known as **Lords-and-Ladies, Soldier's Diddies, Priest's Pintle**. Various names for this plant playfully reference its visual resemblance to male and female genitalia. The symbol of ardor is inspired by the phallic spadix of the plant, which actually self-generates heat. Some species are even known to melt their way through snow.

Ash

GRANDEUR

According to Norse mythology, a massive ash called Yggdrasil holds up the universe. The trembling of this tree of life is said to signal that Ragnarök, the fateful destruction of the world, is on its way. An old superstitious British ritual was to pass children through the split trunk of an ash tree. It was believed that any disorders that they suffered from would be cured. Another ancient English tradition was to feed a spoonful of ash sap to newborn babies before they left their mother's bed for the first time. This was said to offer protection from infant mortality.

ASTER

ASH

ASPHODEL

FLOWERS AND THEIR MEANINGS \

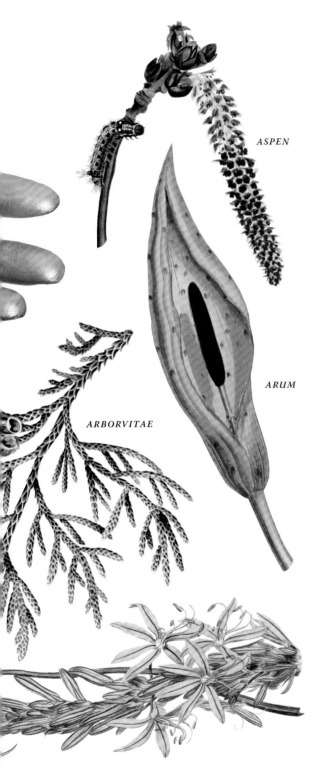

ASPEN

ARUM

ARBORVITAE

Aspen

LAMENTATION

The leaves of the aspen tree tremble due to flattened stalks that attach each leaf to the stem. This movement has been compared to that of women's tongues wagging with gossip and complaints.

Asphodel

MY REGRETS WILL FOLLOW YOU TO THE GRAVE

Asphodel is often planted on graves. Its connection to death originates in Greek mythology: Persephone, goddess of vegetation, wore a crown of the flower. She and her husband, Hades, ruled the underworld, which encompassed the Asphodel Meadows. This part of the underworld was where the spirits of regular people were sent after death.

Aster

AFTERTHOUGHT

Also known as **Michaelmas Daisy**. Asteria, a Titan goddess from Greek mythology, ruled over shooting stars and nighttime divinations. When she scattered stardust, starburst-shaped asters would bloom where the specks landed. She lives on in the night sky as part of the constellation of Virgo.

China Aster
Variety

Double Aster
I share your sentiments

Auricula

PAINTING

Also known as **Bear's Ears**. Hailing from the mountainous regions of central Europe, auricula leaves share a similar shape to that of a bear's ears. It was once believed that the cheerful auricula flourished on animal blood. Raw pieces of meat were often placed by its roots when the buds were just starting to form to ensure large, full blossoms.

Scarlet Auricula
Avarice

Yellow Auricula
Splendor

Autumn Crocus

MY BEST DAYS ARE PAST

Also known as **Meadow Saffron, Naked Ladies**. Despite its name and resemblance to the crocus, this toxic flower does not produce saffron. Nineteenth-century nurse Catherine Wilson was a serial murderer with at least seven victims. After convincing patients to write her into their wills, she would poison them with a liquid preparation of autumn crocus. In 1862, she made history as the last woman to be publicly hanged in London. A crowd of twenty thousand spectators showed up to witness the event.

AZALEA

AUTUMN CROCUS

Azalea

TEMPERANCE

Azalea shrubs, which are a subspecies of rhododendron, were first cultivated for prestigious samurai gardens in seventeenth-century Japan. They are connected with the symbol of temperance because they do not thrive in overly fertilized soil. They prefer to take only what they need. In China, the azalea is known as the "thinking of home" bush.

AURICULA

B

Balm of Gilead

CURE; RELIEF

Also known as *Judea, Balm of Mecca*. Named after the region where it was first produced, balm of Gilead was historically treasured as a rare botanical perfume and medicinal ointment. Although most commonly associated with *Commiphora gileadensis*, the Arabian balsam tree, the true botanical source for this oil—which was highly venerated by Jewish, Christian, and Muslim people—is debated to this day.

Balsam Apple

A CRITIC

The balsam apple plant bears a straggly vine with tendrils, pale yellow flowers, and orange warty fruits that burst open to reveal sticky scarlet seeds. Some have described the fruit as so ugly that it's beautiful. The seeds and ripe fruit are quite poisonous. The boiled plant is sometimes mixed with witch hazel or isopropyl alcohol as a topical antiseptic to treat blisters and sores from insect bites and herpes.

Barberry

SOURNESS OF TEMPER

The barberry flower is often considered to exhibit traits similar to an ill-tempered person. The shrub is full of thorns and sour berries. In response to the slightest physical contact, the flower reacts with great irritation and all its stamens fold around the pistil.

Basil

HATRED

Ancient Greek and Roman culture connected this aromatic herb to hate, poverty, and misfortune. Superstition insists that curses such as "hate has the eye of the basilisk" should be spoken aloud anytime someone first sows these seeds. In medieval times, it was discovered that basil couldn't thrive when planted next to rue, a plant believed to be an enemy to poisons. Basil was then believed to be poisonous. The French phrase *semer le basilic*, which translates to "sowing basil," has come to mean slander or sowing discord.

BALM OF GILEAD

BASIL

BALSAM APPLE

BARBERRY

Bay Laurel

GLORY

In ancient Greece and Rome, bay laurel was associated with accomplishment. Roman generals would send dispatches of victory to the senate called laureate letters, because they were enclosed in laurel leaves. It is said that Julius Caesar loved the privilege of wearing a crown of laurels because it hid his baldness.

Bay Leaf
I change but in death

Bee Balm

YOUR WHIMS ARE QUITE UNBEARABLE

Also known as **Bergamot, Horsemint**. A balm tends to indicate consolation, soothing, and solace. Many Native American cultures have used bee balm medicinally. The Niitsitapi (Blackfoot) people of the North American Great Plains in particular identified the balm's antiseptic properties. This plant is a natural source for thymol, which is used as the active ingredient in many commercial mouthwashes.

Beech

PROSPERITY

As soon as a deer or other woodland creature begins nibbling on beech bark, the tree releases tannins that have an unpleasant taste. The delicate bark does not heal itself, so carvings (such as lovers' initials) never go away. Early European settlers in America used to gather beech leaves to stuff their mattresses, and the bed fillings would not need to be refreshed or changed for eight years.

BEE BALM

BEECH

BELLFLOWER

BELLADONNA

Belladonna

SILENCE

Also known as **Deadly Nightshade**. There are many accounts from the medieval era of a special witches' concoction including belladonna. Deadly nightshade would be combined with other herbal elements as well as rendered animal fat to create a botanical ointment. Folklore tells of witches who would smear the potent grease onto their household broomsticks before pressing the staff between their legs as a way to pleasure themselves. Witches were occasionally caught galloping around, having absorbed the intoxicant through their vaginal mucous membranes, high off self-pleasure. This is how the notion of witches flying on broomsticks was derived.

Bellflower

CONSTANCY

The name bellflower can be used to describe any of the more than five hundred species in the *Campanula* genus. The roots and leaves of the rampion bellflower are enjoyed as an edible vegetable. Salad herbs were not commonly cultivated in sixteenth-century England, so when King Henry VIII and Queen Catherine were in the mood for a salad, someone had to go all the way to Flanders, Belgium, to fetch some.

White Bellflower
Gratitude

BAY LAUREL

Belvedere

I DECLARE AGAINST YOU

If a brutal rainstorm or intense gale of wind detaches a dried-out belvedere plant from its roots, it becomes a tumbleweed. The straggly ball of dried stems rolls around, propelled by the breeze, releasing seeds along the way.

Betony

SURPRISE

Betony has been used as a cure-all for issues such as premenstrual syndrome and frayed nerves. Fresh betony can be intoxicating when eaten, leading to extravagant and impulsive actions. When prepared as a dried snuff to ease the pain of headaches, it causes frequent sneezing.

Bilberry

TREACHERY

The brightly colored berries of the bilberry shrub are often connected to Pele, the Hawaiian goddess of fire and volcanoes. In Hawaii, it was common to throw bilberry branches into a volcanic crater as an offering to the goddess before daring to eat the dark fruit.

BILBERRY

BIRCH

BINDWEED

BELVEDERE

BETONY

Bindweed

BONDS

Also known as **Convolvulus, *Old Man's Night Cap*.** The clinging bindweed vine is almost impossible to eradicate once it introduces itself into a hedge. It insists on twisting away from the sun. If forcibly wrapped to face the sun, the vine will correct its course or die.

Blue Bindweed
Extinguishing hopes

Great Bindweed
Dangerous insinuation

Night Bindweed
Night

Pink Bindweed
Worth sustained by judicious and tender affection

Birch

MEEKNESS

The old English proverb "Birchen twigs break no bones" is inspired by the slender and supple branches of the birch tree. In Upper Brittany, superstition led believers to place oven-dried birch leaves in the cots of weak infants. This practice was believed to bring a baby strength. The inner bark of the birch tree contains a resin that has waterproof qualities and helps resist decay. Indigenous peoples from northern locations around the globe have used the wood from this tree to make shelters, canoes, buckets, and utensils.

Birdsfoot Trefoil

REVENGE

Also known as **Eggs and Bacon**. The yolk-yellow blossoms of this flowering plant are topped with bits of orange—the look of which has been compared to breakfast food. The international symbols for radiation, biohazard, and fallout shelter—designed in mid-twentieth-century America—all stem from the three-leaf trefoil shape.

Bittersweet Nightshade

TRUTH

Also known as **Woody Nightshade**. A climbing vine, bittersweet nightshade displays vivid purple flowers and clusters of luscious red berries. These berries smell dangerously similar to their botanical cousin, the tomato, but they are poisonous to humans. Throughout the Middle Ages, the plant was associated with witchcraft and lore. It was a common practice to hang a sachet of plant matter around the neck of a cow to protect it from evil. Placed under a pillow, the vine was thought to mend a broken heart, while an amulet made from the berries was believed to repel malicious gossip.

*BITTERSWEET
NIGHTSHADE*

*BLACK-EYED
SUSAN*

*BLACKBERRY
BLOSSOM*

*BIRDSFOOT
TREFOIL*

Blackberry Blossom

ENVY

Also known as **Bramble**. Juicy blackberries grow on densely barbed bushes. A British old wives' tale tells of young children who refused to learn to walk being forced to crawl through blackberry bushes as punishment. This ritual was intended to inspire children to stand up and walk away from the painful prickles. Another British superstition prohibited blackberry consumption after September 29. It was believed that Lucifer had been cast out of heaven on this day, plummeting to earth and landing in a barbed blackberry bramble. The devil was believed to curse the plant every year, bringing bad luck, illness, or death to those who eat its fruit after September 29.

Black-Eyed Susan

JUSTICE

Also known as **Rudbeckia**. A member of the sunflower family, this golden bloom with its signature dark, domed center has been used in various traditional medicines. An ooze collected from the roots has been used by the Anigiduwagi (Cherokee) as a remedy for earaches. The tender leaves of sochan, an edible cousin of the black-eyed Susan, is an important green featured in Cherokee cuisine.

Blackthorn

DIFFICULTY

According to Irish folklore, blackthorn bushes are guarded by a tribe of fairies known as the Lunantishees. Any person who dared to cut a blackthorn's branches or wear its flowers on November 11 or May 11 would be cursed. Offerings of cake, milk, and ale were believed to win the fairies' favor.

Bladder Nut

FRIVOLOUS AMUSEMENT

Children love to play with the whoopie cushion–like bladder nut: when squeezed, the nuts erupt with a humorous flatulent noise. In the country of Georgia, the buds of this deciduous shrub are seasoned, preserved in brine, and served as a tasty dish.

Bleeding Heart

FLY WITH ME

Also known as **Venus's Car, Little Boy's Breeches, Lady in a Bath**. Bleeding heart is native to northern China, Korea, and Japan and is treasured for its pink-and-white heart-shaped flowers. Superstition says that if you crush a bleeding heart and the juice is red, your love is reciprocated. If the juice is white, it is not reciprocated.

BLUET

BLADDER NUT

BLACKTHORN

Bluebell

CONSTANCY

The common bluebell thrives in western Europe's ancient woodland, with patches of the flower often serving as indicators to identify old-growth forests. The British bluebell is protected by the U.K. Wildlife and Countryside Act. To uproot this flower from its natural habitat or to participate in the trade of its bulbs or seeds is a criminal offense. Fines can run as high as £5,000 per illegally plucked bulb.

Bluet

CONTENT

Also known as **Houstonia**, *Quaker Ladies*. These tiny woodland flowers are sometimes confused for forget-me-nots. The four-petaled blooms are called Quaker ladies because they are reminiscent of the pale blue-and-white fabrics and bonnets Quaker women once wore. A bluet infusion was used by the Anigiduwagi (Cherokee) people as a cure for bed-wetting. The Diné (Navajo) Nation used a pink variety of red bluet to soothe menstrual issues.

*BLEEDING
HEART*

BLUEBELL

Borage

BLUNTNESS

In the *Odyssey*, Homer describes a special wine known as nepenthe as a magical potion that dissolves all sorrows with forgetfulness. Some suspect the drink was laced with opium, but Pliny the Elder, the Roman naturalist and philosopher, believed the potion was borage flower muddled into wine. In the nineteenth century, Charles Dickens served his guests "cider cup," a drink containing cider, brandy, sherry, and borage. An old folktale suggests that slipping borage into a lover's drink might give them the courage to propose.

Box

STOICISM

Wood from the box tree is firm and does not warp. Though there are many theories about the wood that made up Christ's cross, it is often depicted in paintings as box tree wood. Old folktales describe the box tree as an effective security measure against flower-stealing witches, who apparently cannot resist the urge to count the tree's leaves. In such dense foliage, witches are doomed to start counting over again and again.

Broom

HUMILITY

St. Louis of France chose the flower from this evergreen shrub as an emblem for his new order of knighthood. The protective league comprised one hundred nobles. The yellow broom flower was emblazoned on the collars of these knights alongside the motto *Deus exaltat humiles*, meaning "God exalts the humble."

BOX

BORAGE

BRYONY

BUCKBEAN

BROOM

BUGLOSS

Bryony

PROSPERITY

Also known as **Our Lady's Seal**. The bryony is a climbing plant that features greenish-white flowers and bright red berries. Its thick, pale root conforms to the shape of any pot. Long ago, roots that had been manipulated into outlandish forms were exhibited as freak curiosities. Sometimes bryony root was molded into a humanoid embodiment that could be mistaken for the more valuable mandrake root. It would be sold under false pretenses to reap great profit.

Black Bryony
Be my support, my stay

Buckbean

CALM REPOSE

Also known as **Bogbean**. Growing in bogs or other shallow water conditions, these distinctly hairy, star-shaped blossoms have been described as appearing to float in a calm repose. Used in traditional Chinese medicine to treat insomnia and restlessness, this consciousness-calming plant is known as **sleeping herb**.

Bugloss

FALSEHOOD

Bugloss flowers are a neon bluish purple, but the roots are used to make red pigment. The alternate name **alkanet** originates from the Arabic *alhinna* or *henna*, which describes the reddish dye derived from the Egyptian privet plant, used to decorate hands and feet. Frenchwomen once used a powdered preparation of this plant as a cosmetic to give themselves a rosy glow.

Burdock

IMPORTUNITY; TOUCH ME NOT

The prickly seed capsules of burdock stick to animals and clothing. Finding a bunch of these fishhook burrs stuck to his own wool socks, as well as his dog's fur, after walking in the Alps, the Swiss engineer George de Mestral was inspired to invent Velcro. The name of this temporary fastener is a portmanteau of the French words for velvet (*velours*) and hook (*croché*).

Buttercup

CHILDISHNESS

For hundreds of years, children have playfully held buttercups under their chins as a form of specific fortune-telling: If the yellow hue glows on the skin of your chin, you must like butter. The reflective abilities are due to the unique cellular structure of the flower. The surface of a buttercup bounces light with such intensity that it can be compared to glass. This botanical ability is put to good use attracting pollinators. The claim that butter gets its golden color from cows who graze on buttercups is false. In fact, cows do not eat this plant at all; it is bitter and toxic, causing blisters to animals who eat it.

Hairy Buttercup
Irony

BUTTERFLY WEED

Butterfly Weed

LET ME GO

Also known as **Orange Milkweed, Butterfly Love**. This colorful species of milkweed is named for the butterfly because of its plentiful nectar. It is a favored food source for monarch butterflies, a variety of moths, hummingbirds, bees, and other insects. Native Americans and European settlers boiled the roots of this plant as a treatment for diarrhea and respiratory issues. Candlewicks were also spun from the downy seedpods.

BURDOCK

BUTTERCUP

CALLA LILY

CABBAGE
BLOSSOM

CACTUS

C

Cabbage Blossom

PROFIT

Items of necessity to the masses, such as the cabbage, turned large profits for merchants. Famed seventeenth-century French gardener André Le Nôtre was bestowed a rank of nobility after planting the gardens of Versailles, the Tuileries, and the area that would later become the Champs-Élysées. His coat of arms features a large cabbage with three slugs.

Cactus

WARMTH

A gifted cactus passionately suggests "I burn for you." The spines are known to pierce, much like Cupid's arrow. There are 1,750 species of cacti in existence—some of which can grow to be fifty feet tall. Centuries old, they are sometimes considered monumental landmarks.

Creeping Cactus
Horror

Prickly Pear Cactus
Satire

Calla Lily

MAGNIFICENT BEAUTY

Neither a calla nor a lily, the elegant calla lily was championed by the aesthetic art movement of the late nineteenth century. Adherents to the adage "art for art's sake," creatives were more interested in surrounding themselves with beauty than searching for deeper meaning. With this philosophy in mind, Oscar Wilde was known to decorate his dining table with calla lilies and sunflowers.

Camellia

UNPRETENDING EXCELLENCE

Coco Chanel loved the camellia flower specifically because it bore no scent. The fashion designer would pin a bloom to her jacket, and it would not interfere with her signature fragrance, Chanel No. 5. Camellia scented cosmetics do exist, but they are based on "fantasy notes"—synthetic fragrances that have been invented to evoke the visual beauty of the flower.

Camellia japonica
My heart bleeds for you

White Camellia
Perfected loveliness

Campion

SNARE

Also known as **Catchfly, Bloody William**. The campion has been cultivated for British gardens for more than seven hundred years. In the early 2010s, frozen seeds—estimated thirty-two thousand years old—were discovered in the permafrost of Siberia. Presumably, they had been burrowed by an Ice Age squirrel. The plant turned out to be a specific strain of campion that had been extinct; it was resurrected by Russian scientists in 2012.

Red Campion
Youthful love

Rose Campion
Only you deserve my love

White Campion
I fall into the trap laid for me

CANTERBURY BELL

CAMPION

CANNABIS

CANDYTUFT

CAMELLIA

Candytuft

ARCHITECTURE

Also known as **Iberis**. The name candytuft is not connected to sweet desserts but was named after the city of Candia (now Heraklion) on the island of Crete. The white, pink, or purple blooms grow in layers along a stalk, which sometimes resemble an architectural column or a building made up of several stories.

Cannabis

FATE

The psychoactive drug known as **marijuana** is derived from the flowering cannabis plant. During the nineteenth century, the drug was widely available in pharmacies for medicinal use, and candies such as "the Arabian gum of enchantment" were sold in New York City general stores. By 1906, many states started restricting access to marijuana as a recreational drug. By 1970, cannabis was firmly outlawed across the United States. One year later, a bag of marijuana was sold over a primitive version of the internet. This deal—between Stanford and MIT students—was the first commercial transaction to ever be facilitated online.

Canterbury Bell

ACKNOWLEDGMENT

This flower was named for twelfth-century English pilgrims who carried little bells as they walked through fields of wildflowers on their way to the St. Thomas Becket shrine in Canterbury. In Persian, the flower is known as *gol-e estekani*, which means "glass flower" due to its resemblance to a small drinking glass.

63

FLOWERS AND THEIR MEANINGS

Cape Marigold

FOREKNOWLEDGE

Also known as **The Weather Prophet, African Moon Flower**, Dimorphotheca. This sun-loving flower from South Africa helps with weather forecasting since it tends to close up before a rainstorm begins. The seeds are harvested for their high concentration of dimorphecolic acid, which is useful in the manufacturing of resins, varnishes, and industrial foams.

Cardamine

PATERNAL ERROR

Also known as **Cuckoo Flower, Lady's Smock, Mayflower**. Shakespeare's King Lear adorns himself with a crown of *Cardamine* after forsaking his regal diadem. The bloom was considered sacred in the realm of the fairies; bringing these pinkish blooms indoors or using them in May Day garlands was thought to bring bad luck.

Cardinal Flower

DISTINCTION

The cardinal flower shares the same vivid red hue of the traditional garments worn by Roman Catholic cardinals. Native to the Americas, these flowers are used by the Zuni people to make *schumaakwe* cakes, which can be used as topical treatments to ease rheumatism and swelling.

CARNATION

CARDINAL FLOWER

CAPE MARIGOLD

RED CARNATION

CARDAMINE

Carnation

STRONG AND PURE LOVE

See page 66.
Known as *el clavel* in Spanish, the carnation has been incorporated into many aspects of the country's culture. It is customary for single women to wear a red carnation behind their ear; red carnations are thrown into the bullfighting ring after a matador defeats a bull; and the style of ruffled sevillana dresses worn by flamenco dancers were designed to look like carnations.

Mixed-Colors Carnation
Pride and beauty

Pink Carnation
Woman's love

Red Carnation
Pure and ardent love

Striped Carnation
Refusal

White Carnation
Young girl

Yellow Carnation
Disdain

Carnation

STRONG AND PURE LOVE

See page 65

A single carnation worn on the lapel is a classic menswear accessory. Available in a plethora of colors, the carnation takes on different roles as a badge or signifier of identity, depending on the hue. At the University of Oxford, for example, it is customary for students to wear a carnation as they take exams. Students wear a white carnation during their first exam, pink for all the intermediate exams, and red for their final.

The twenty-fifth president of the United States, William McKinley, was given a red carnation by a friend and political opponent when they both ran for Congress in Ohio in 1876. After winning the race, McKinley developed a superstition about red carnations and always wore one on his lapel. As president, a vase full of red carnations was always on display in the Oval Office.

In 1901, McKinley was greeting people in Buffalo, New York, when a little girl asked for a flower. With none on hand, he did something he never did. He unpinned the carnation from his own lapel and gave it to her. Moments later, he was shot in the abdomen. He died eight days later, leaving Vice President Theodore Roosevelt to succeed him. Ohio designated the carnation the official state flower in his honor.

Writer and Victorian-era dandy Oscar Wilde is often associated with the green carnation. In 1892 he instructed his entourage to wear the flowers in their buttonholes to the opening of his play *Lady Windemere's Fan*. The technique to dye fresh-cut flowers by plunging the stem in colored water was first developed by Alfred Nesbit only ten years earlier. When asked the significance of the unusually hued flower, Wilde coyly answered, "Nothing whatever, but that is just what nobody will guess." Though Wilde's true intentions were never confirmed, at the time English society speculated that the green flower was a symbol for homosexuality. By proudly wearing this unnatural bloom, some thought Wilde was mocking the societal condemnation of what was considered to be an "unnatural love."

When the anonymously written novel *The Green Carnation* was published two years after the opening of Wilde's play (to much scandal and success!), it was assumed that Wilde was the author. The main characters closely resemble Oscar Wilde and his lover, the young poet Lord Alfred Douglas, and the green carnation is worn by men who subscribe to "the higher philosophy."

Despite refuting authorship in a letter to the *Pall Mall Gazette*, the book was used as evidence against him in court. Faced with charges of homosexuality, he was found guilty and sentenced to two years in prison with hard labor. Later, it was revealed that the novel had been written by Robert Hichens. "I invented that magnificent flower," Wilde said. "But with the middle-class and mediocre book that usurps its strangely beautiful name I have, I need hardly say, nothing whatsoever to do. The Flower is a work of Art. The book is not."

Carolina Allspice

BENEVOLENCE

Also known as **Calycanthus**, **_Eastern Sweet Shrub_**, **_Spice Bush_**. The fragrant Carolina allspice smells like strawberries or apples and is often compared to a lobster trap. The petals on this flower align to allow easy access to pollinating beetles while simultaneously blocking their exit. It is only after the insect has completed its pollen business that the inner petals will bend back, allowing escape.

Cattail

INDISCRETION

Cattails typically grow in water that is about three feet deep, with the flowering stalks reaching as high as ten feet tall. The shoots of this wetland reed, which are known in Russia as **_Cossack's asparagus_**, can be picked and eaten. The taste is described as a cross between a cucumber and a zucchini. In the nineteenth century, miners dipped cattails in beeswax or oil and set them ablaze to use as torches.

CEDAR

CHAMOMILE

CAROLINA ALLSPICE

CATTAIL

CENTAURY

Cedar

STRENGTH

The coniferous cedar tree has dependably provided durable wood for thousands of years. The fragrant oils found in cedar trunks are a natural moth repellent. The wood itself absorbs moisture and can prevent rot, making it a popular choice for chests of drawers and other furniture pieces meant for storage. A variety of cedar species are also used for the casing of leaded pencils.

Cedar Leaf
I live for thee

Cedar of Lebanon
Incorruptible

Centaury

FELICITY

Also known as *Feverwort,* **Centaurium**. Common centaury is named after Chiron, the centaur from Greek mythology known for his expertise in herbal medicines. The pink flower has a long history of being used as a fever reducer as well as a treatment for snakebites. During the Middle Ages, these small star-shaped flowers were thought to provide protection from evil spirits.

Chamomile

ENERGY IN ADVERSITY

The sweet fragrance of chamomile is similar to that of an apple, so it is not surprising to learn that the daisy-like flower's name comes from the Greek for "earth apple." When dried and infused with hot water, the flower is well loved as a relaxing nighttime drink. It is said that gamblers used to wash their hands with this floral tea, hoping it would bestow some good luck.

Chaste Tree

TO LIVE WITHOUT LOVE

In ancient Greece, stems and leaves of the chaste tree were used as bedding by the women of Athens during Thesmophoria, a time when they left their husbands to participate in rituals of chastity. It was believed to have properties capable of tamping down lustful urges.

Cherry Blossom

SPIRITUAL BEAUTY

See page 72.
The goddess of Mount Fuji, Konohanasakuya-hime, whose name translates as "tree-blossom-blooming princess," is a figure from Japanese mythology who is closely connected to volcanoes and sakura, or cherry blossoms. Shinto shrines built in her honor appear on Mount Fuji to appease the volcano and avoid eruptions.

Cherry
Good education

Cherry Laurel

PERFIDY

The Roman emperor Nero used cherry laurel, which contains hydrocyanic acid, to poison his enemy's wells. In modern times, there have been instances where gardeners, who are unaware of the cherry laurel's poisonous properties, have loaded up their cars with trimmings to take to a dump or compost only to find themselves falling asleep at the wheel because of the gaseous emissions.

CHESTNUT TREE

CHERVIL

CHERRY BLOSSOM

CHERRY LAUREL

CHASTE TREE

Chervil

SINCERITY

Chervil grows in delicate umbrella-shaped clusters of tiny white blooms. During the Middle Ages, this flavorful spring herb was consumed as a cure for the hiccups, and the boiled roots were believed to protect against the plague.

Chestnut Tree

DO ME JUSTICE

Chestnuts have been farmed by humans for about four thousand years. The nut of this tree is an important part of the diet for Indigenous peoples hailing from the Eastern Woodlands region of North America. In addition to enjoying the sweet and starchy source of protein, the Lenni Lenape have used chestnuts to catch fish. When ground chestnut—which they refer to as *opim*—is sprinkled onto stream water, it makes fish dizzy and easier to harvest.

Cherry
Blossoms

SPIRITUAL
BEAUTY

See page 70

Every spring, for about two weeks, cherry trees bloom into fluffy pink clouds before the blossoms softly fall like confetti. In Japan, the principle of *mono no aware,* which translates to "a sensitivity to ephemera" or "an empathy toward things," is often used to describe this beautiful show of impermanence. Since the third century CE, the practice of watching blossoms (called *hanami*) has been the nationally observed celebration of *sakura*—or cherry blossom—season.

By 1639, Japan had created an isolationist foreign policy, effectively cutting off the country from other cultures for more than two centuries. When this policy ended in 1853, Japanese imports flourished. Motifs such as the cherry blossom appeared in many western European paintings, in decor, and on trendy handheld fans.

The most produced variety of edible cherries in America is the Bing cherry. The fruit is named after the Chinese foreman who played a key role in its cultivation and development. Ah Bing, a Manchurian immigrant, began working at Lewelling Orchard in Oregon in the late 1850s, planting, breeding, and growing a variety of cherry trees. Seth Lewelling and Bing worked together for many years, and in 1875 one of the crossbred cherry trees under his care bore the fruit we know today as the Bing cherry.

Natural disasters, political troubles, and famine in China inspired hundreds of thousands of men to cross the Pacific in search of opportunities in America. In the midst of the American Civil War, when so many men were off fighting, Chinese immigrants worked as farmers, miners, and laborers but were paid a meager wage. There were racist and xenophobic complaints that these men were stealing American jobs; violence was often inflicted on them. In 1882, the Chinese Exclusion Act barred the immigration of Chinese laborers.

During periods of anti-Chinese riots and violence, Bing and other Chinese workers were able to take shelter in Lewelling's home. Over the years, Bing sent his wages back to his wife and children in China. In 1889, he returned to his homeland to visit his family and never returned. It is possible that he was refused reentry because of the Exclusion Act, or perhaps he no longer felt safe living in the United States.

Chickweed

RENDEZVOUS

While a coded bouquet was a seductive way to suggest a rendezvous, it was best to establish a meeting's day and time in a more reliable manner. According to John Wesley Hanson's *Flora's Dial, a flower dedicated to each day of the year* (1846), chickweed specifically signifies May 2, and mouse-eared chickweed represents April 5. John Henry Ingram's *Flora symbolica* (1869) offers March 4 and March 2 instead.

Mouse-Eared Chickweed
Ingenious simplicity

Chicory

FRUGALITY

When New Orleans was founded in 1718, its location and easy trade access made coffee crops an integral part of the city's culture. France established coffee plantations in Haiti and Cuba. After the Boston Tea Party in 1773, American colonists developed a taste for coffee. When shipments were blocked during the Civil War, locals began mixing roasted chicory root with ground coffee to stretch out their supply. Chicory-blend coffee has become a cherished drink, enjoyed to this day at the famous Café du Monde and elsewhere in New Orleans.

CHINABERRY

CHICORY

CHICKWEED

CHRYSANTHEMUM

Chinaberry

DISSENSION

Also known as **Pride of India, Persian Lilac, Bead Tree**. Although the cherry-like fruit of this tree is poisonous, the pits are used as jewelry beads in many parts of the world, including Botswana and India, where chinaberry is believed to prevent infectious diseases. Chinaberry is used by the Umonhon (Omaha) people of the American Midwest—they consider the pits good luck. The wood of this tree is also carved for Islamic prayer beads.

Chrysanthemum

CHEERFULNESS UNDER ADVERSITY

This flower been cultivated in China since at least 1500 BCE. The Chongyang, or Chrysanthemum, Festival started during the Han dynasty and celebrates the cleansing of negative energy from both house and body. One tradition is to drink chrysanthemum wine. The autumnal flower is believed to hold yang energy and attract good luck into the home. In Chinese, chrysanthemum *(juhua)* sounds similar to *jiu*, which means "long enduring." When the flower is paired with branches of pine, it suggests long life.

Red Chrysanthemum
I love

White Chrysanthemum
Truth

Yellow Chrysanthemum
Slighted love

Cilantro

CONCEALED MERIT

Also known as **coriander**, cilantro is one of the oldest herbs actively in use today. Used as an ingredient in cuisines around the globe, coriander has a divisive flavor. Because of a variation in human olfactory receptor genes, cilantro tastes strangely soapy for a small percentage of people, while for most, the green has a deliciously bright flavor.

Cinnamon

CHASTITY

Originally derived from the bark of Sri Lankan trees, cinnamon is loved around the globe for its distinct flavor and aroma. For medieval Europeans, the origin of the spice remained a mystery. In 1248, King Louis IX, and others venturing out on the Seventh Crusade from France to Egypt, fell for tales that cinnamon (along with ginger, aloe, and rhubarb) was dredged up with fishing nets from the Nile, out near the edge of the world. In 1306, Giovanni da Montecorvino, an Italian missionary traveling in South Asia, identified the source that traders had kept secret for so long. The Portuguese, Dutch, French, and English soon took turns invading Ceylon in order to harvest their own cinnamon supply.

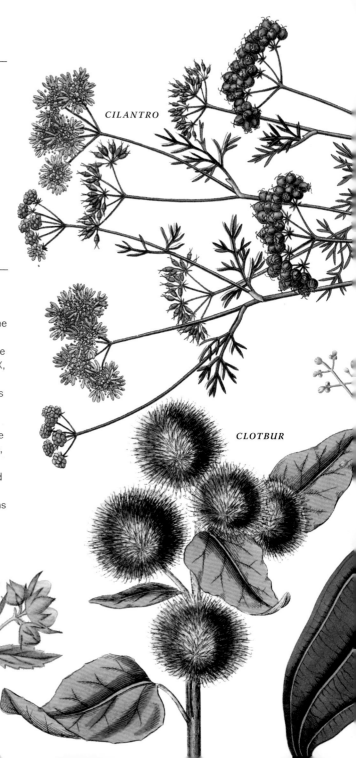

CILANTRO

CLOTBUR

CINQUEFOIL

FLOWERS AND THEIR MEANINGS \

CLEMATIS

CINNAMON

Cinquefoil

BELOVED DAUGHTER

The name *cinquefoil* describes the five-petaled yellow flower accompanied by five-part leaves. When included in heraldry, the cinquefoil is emblematic of power, honor, and loyalty. The floral form appears in ecclesiastical architecture as far back as 1033 in Burgundy, France. According to the language of flowers, "beloved daughter" reflects the plant's protective impulse. When it rains, the leaves fold over the flowers to protect them from harm.

Clematis

MENTAL BEAUTY; ARTIFICE

The clematis is a flowering climbing vine. In ancient Rome, beggars were known to rub the sap of the varietal *Clematis vitalba* on their skin to cause blisters. These fake ulcers were intended to elicit pity; however, they often developed into real sores.

Evergreen Clematis
Poverty

Clematis vitalba
Safety

Clotbur

RUDENESS

The clotbur is not a useful plant. Often confused with burdock, it is rough and prickly with spines and is not particularly beautiful. The hooked spikes of the burrs attach onto fur, and roaming animals help disperse the seeds. With the ability to float, the burrs can also travel to new destinations by water. No matter how carefully it is eradicated from a field, clotbur has a sneaky way of coming back.

Clover

INDUSTRY

Also known as **Shamrock**. A favorite pollinator for industrious honeybees, the clover was a popular symbol in romantic nineteenth-century valentines. Soft patches of the sweet-smelling leaflets created enticing resting spots for lovers to lie down. Druids believed the clover to be a protective charm against evil. Legend says that St. Patrick, when attempting to indoctrinate converts, used the triple leaflets of this plant to explain the Holy Trinity. The first known English reference to the lucky four-leaved clover is from *The Gospelles of Dystaues*, written anonymously in 1507. Whoever finds a four-leaf clover and keeps it reverently, the book states, "shall be ryche all his life."

Four-Leaf Clover
Be mine

Purple Clover
Provident

White Clover
Think of me

COLTSFOOT

CLOVER

FOUR-LEAF CLOVER

CLOVES

COCKSCOMB

Cloves

DIGNITY

The name of the aromatic clove is likely derived from *clou,* the French word for "nail." The spice itself looks like the types of spikes that were used to nail Jesus to the cross. In 200 BCE, Javanese diplomats traveling to China in the time of the Han Dynasty held cloves in their mouths to be assured that their breath would smell nice while they were meeting with the emperor. In 1880, clove cigarettes were invented in Indonesia by Haji Djamhari as a potential cure for his chest pains. Like tobacco, inhaling clove smoke is bad for your health. The cigarettes are known as *kretek,* which is an onomatopoeia for the sound of the cloves crackling as they burn.

Cockscomb

FOPPERY

Cockscomb is named for its visual similarity to a rooster's fanciful headpiece. The colorful, undulating bloom is also known as **velvet flower** in Mexico. In Nigeria, where the leaves are enjoyed as an edible green, the flower is known as *sokoyokoto,* which means "make husbands fat and happy" in Yoruba.

Coltsfoot

JUSTICE SHALL BE DONE

Named for its hoof-shaped leaves, coltsfoot is crowned with soft tufts that look similar to dandelions. Recognized as a medicinal herb, eighteenth-century apothecaries in Paris used to paint coltsfoot signage on their doorposts. Its alternate Latin name, *tussilago,* comes from *tussis dispello,* meaning "cough dispeller."

Columbine

FOLLY

According to Charles Darwin, the name *columbine* stems from the Latin for "dove" because of the flower's resemblance to a nest of hungry baby birds. The flower has also been likened to a jester's hat, which is perhaps where the Victorian interpretation of "folly" came from.

Purple Columbine
Resolved to win

Red Columbine
Anxious and trembling

Corchorus

IMPATIENT OF ABSENCE

Also known as **Jute, Jew's Mallow, Egyptian Spinach**. Some say *Corchorus* is known as Jew's mallow because it was used as an emollient and food by Jewish people in ancient times. Others say it is because the flowering herb is widely dispersed, like a migrating diaspora. It is rumored that a nutritious juice or soup made from these leaves was Cleopatra's antiaging beauty secret.

Coreopsis

ALWAYS CHEERFUL

Also known as **Tickseed**. *Coreopsis* gets its name from the Greek words meaning "bedbug." The little flat fruits of this flower look like bugs. Early American colonists stuffed *Coreopsis* into their mattresses with the belief that it would ward off bedbugs.

Coreopsis arkansa
Love at first sight

COREOPSIS

CORN

CORCHORUS

PURPLE COLUMBINE

CORNCOCKLE

COLUMBINE

Corn

RICHES

When corn was first introduced to Europe in 1735, it was given to people living in poverty who quickly developed pellagra—a disease caused by niacin deficiency. These sleepless people, who couldn't eat regular food and whose pale skin blistered in the sun, may have been the inspiration for vampire stories. Native Americans knew to add slaked lime or calcium hydroxide to their corn in order to absorb the vegetable's niacin. The European settlers did not.

Corncockle

GENTILITY

Also known as **Bastard Nigella**. An old English rhyme "full of weeds and cockle seeds" describes the consequences of a garden run wild. In 2014, when a BBC television show sent viewers complimentary packets of wild corncockle seeds, scandal erupted. It turns out the attractive flower is poisonous (although there is little evidence of the plant causing serious harm unless consumed in very large quantities). The uproar was instigated by someone who spotted a troop of Brownies tending to a patch of these petite purple blooms. Local officials immediately mowed down the flowers and fenced off the area.

Cornflower

DELICACY

Also known as **Bachelor's Button**. Queen Louise of Prussia famously hid her children in a field of wild cornflowers while they fled from Napoleon's forces. She wove floral crowns to keep them calm and quiet while taking cover. After the unification of Germany in 1871, the queen's son, Kaiser Wilhelm I, made his favorite bloom—the cornflower—a national symbol for Germany. In the 1930s and '40s, the Prussian blue blossom was worn by Nazis on their lapels as a covert way to identify each other.

Coronilla

SUCCESS CROWNS YOUR WISHES

Also known as **Crown Vetch**. Each stem of this flower is crowned with a circular cluster of bright yellow blooms. Swedish botanist Carl Linnaeus observed that the blooms of *Coronilla* emit a fragrance throughout the day that can be compared to sweet peas, but they become practically scentless at night.

Cowslip

WINNING GRACE

Cowslip is quite literally named for cow slop, as the fragrant springtime flowers originally grew near bovine dung. The Druids valued the flower and it was used in many magic potions. A cowslip concoction was often paired with other remedies, as cowslip was believed to help with the absorption of other herbs. The drooping yellow flowers were also used to make a slightly narcotic flower wine.

CRANBERRY BLOSSOM

CREPIS

CORONILLA

CRAPE MYRTLE

CORNFLOWER

COWSLIP

Cranberry Blossom

CURE FOR HEARTACHE

In 1550, it was likely the Narragansett people of the Algonquin Nation who introduced these berries, which they knew as *sassamanash*, to European colonists in Massachusetts. Cranberries and other berries—often served with game meat—were a staple in Native American cuisine. Sweetened cranberry sauce was popularized in the nineteenth century and influenced by the jams and jellies fashionable in England at the time.

Crape Myrtle

ELOQUENCE

These crêpe-like crinkly flowers grow in dense clusters on shrub-like trees. Colorful varieties of crape myrtle include Plum Magic, Pink Velour, and Red Rocket. Many cultures believe that by cultivating the crape myrtle flower, peace and love will flourish within your family.

Crepis

PROTECTION

Also known as **Hawk's Beard**. Often called **bearded Crepis,** the buds of these flowers are shielded by leaves covered in bristly dark whiskers. These leaves form a protective "beard" that shelters the bloom from pests, weather, and other types of damage. For species that feature similar protection, the leaves tend to fall away once the flower is mature. Not so for the *Crepis*, whose hairy leaves stick around, supporting the yellow flower until it dies.

Cress

RESOLUTION

Cress was once known by its old Saxon name, *kers*. The sayings "not worth a curse" and "I don't care a curse" may be references to this ubiquitous leafy green. British publications from the fifteenth century describe a variety of magical tonics that predicted whether someone suffering from bloody diarrhea would live or die. Although the recipes vary, they each call for a pennyweight of cress. If the symptoms resolve, survival is likely. If suffering persists, death is imminent. Cress is also used as an herbal remedy for diarrhea by both the Hausa and Zulu peoples of Africa.

Crocus

ABUSE NOT

The thread-like filaments of saffron procured from the crocus flower are, by weight, as valuable as gold. During the reign of King Henry VIII, the rich yellow saffron was used by ladies of the court to dye their hair. The style was so popular that the entire kingdom's saffron supply dwindled. Being his favorite spice, the king forbade use of saffron, threatening severe punishment. In 1556, not long after the king passed away, England had an extreme bumper crop of crocuses and farmers declared, "God did shite saffron."

Spring Crocus
Youthful gladness

CUDWEED

CROCUS

FLOWERS AND THEIR MEANINGS \

CRESS

CROWN IMPERIAL

Crown Imperial

MAJESTY; POWER

The crown imperial is featured in many legends that explain the downturned posture of its bright floral bells. Persian lore describes an extraordinarily beautiful queen whose good looks maddened the king. Without proof, he accused her of infidelity and banished her, leaving her to wander the nearby fields, crying. When she stopped walking, the queen shrank down and took root, transforming into the sad crown imperial flower.

Cudweed

UNCEASING REMEMBRANCE

In Taiwan, dumplings known as *caozaiguo* or *shuquguo* are enjoyed during the Qingming Festival, a holiday celebrated by the Han Chinese and the ethnic Chinese of Malaysia and Singapore. The holiday is also known as Tomb-Sweeping Day, Chinese Memorial Day, or Ancestor's Day. The green treats are prepared with a sweet dough made from glutinous rice and filled with a paste made from Jersey cudweed, a species found on every continent except Antarctica.

Cup and Saucer Vine

GOSSIP

The bell-shaped blossoms on this flowering vine look similar to teacups, and the leaves at the base of each bloom appear to support the "cup," just as a saucer would. These purple or white flowers are emblematic of gossip because of the juicy chatter typically shared during teatime.

CUP AND SAUCER VINE

Currant Blossom

THY FROWN WILL KILL ME

The fruit of the currant plant is generally pleasant but not necessarily a standout among other popular berries. Because of its universal neutrality, a branch of currants is seen to please all. During World War II, when the United Kingdom's access to citrus fruit was cut off, Winston Churchill urged British farmers to grow black currants, which are high in vitamin C. The black currant soft drink Ribena is popular among English people to this day.

Branch of Currants
You please all

Cuscuta

MEANNESS

Also known as **Dodder of Thyme, Strangleweed, Witch's Hair**. *Cuscuta* is a parasitic plant that sucks the life out of other plants. Lacking the ability for proper photosynthesis, this noxious pest climbs onto other plants. The young shoots must locate a host within a week, or they will die. Following scent, the dodder will grow toward a potential victim plant until it can wrap around and sink into it, drinking up nutrients. A field invaded by *Cuscuta* looks like an explosion of Silly String.

Cyclamen

DIFFIDENCE

Cyclamen was a favorite flower of Leonardo da Vinci. He often decorated the margins of his manuscripts with drawings of the frost-hardy bloom and columbine flowers. Sometimes referred to as **swine's bread**, fragrant cyclamen flowers are a favorite snack for hungry pigs.

CURRANT BLOSSOM

CYPRESS

CYPRESS VINE

CUSCUTA

CYCLAMEN

Cypress

DEATH AND ETERNAL SORROW

As an emblem of the underworld, the cypress tree has long been linked to burials and mourning. Its durable wood was used to make chests that held Egyptian mummies and for heroes' coffins in Greece. To announce a death in Victorian England, a wreath made of sweet-smelling cypress mixed with other evergreens was hung on the front door with a black ribbon. The addition of marigolds expressed extreme despair.

Cypress Vine

BUSYBODY

Described as a tender scrambler, the cypress vine is dotted with scarlet, pink, or white tubular flowers. It is a vigorous grower and is frequently visited by hummingbirds. Native to Central America, seeds and specimens were sent to Europe as early as the sixteenth century, where it was popularized as a medicinal plant. For centuries, the cypress vine was thought to be a South Asian plant. Like a game of broken telephone, the origin of the flower was muddled. Europeans were often confused by their own naming system, and many misunderstood the West Indies (a tropical subregion of North American islands) to be East India.

D

Daffodil

SELF-LOVE

Also known as **Narcissus**. The Greek myth of Narcissus tells of a young hunter, known for his beauty, who gazed on his reflection in a pool, transfixed with self-admiration. He had been tricked by Aphrodite into falling in love with his own image, believing it to be someone else. Narcissus died by this pool, and a yellow flower grew from his remains. Thus, narcissism and vanity have since been associated with this flower.

Jonquil
I desire a return of affection

Dahlia

INSTABILITY

The dahlia was named the national flower of Mexico in 1963. The flower's tubers have long been incorporated into Oaxacan cuisine, and an extract from roasted tubers is used to flavor drinks across Central America. Aztecs hollowed out dahlia stems to use for water irrigation. Adored as boldly colorful garden flowers, some varieties feature blooms the size of dinner plates.

A bunch of dahlias
My gratitude exceeds your care

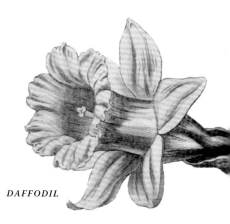

DAFFODIL

DAHLIA

Daisy

INNOCENCE

The name daisy is derived from the Old English *dægeseag*, meaning "day's eye." *Alice's Adventures in Wonderland* by Lewis Carroll begins with a sleepy young Alice trying to decide if she should make a daisy chain—a common amusement for children dating back to medieval times—when the White Rabbit suddenly interrupts her, symbolically sparking her awakened quest for knowledge. Later, she warns a patch of talkative daisies, "If you don't hold your tongues, I'll pick you!"

Double Daisy
I reciprocate your affection

Field Daisy
I will think of it

Ox-Eye Daisy
Patience

Red Daisy
Beauty unknown to the possessor

Dame's Rocket

YOU ARE THE QUEEN OF COQUETTES; FASHION

Blooming in shades of purple and white, dame's rocket looks like phlox. It emits a scent comparable to that of sweet violet and clove—but only in the evening. To lift her spirits, Marie-Antoinette was smuggled bunches of this flower while she was imprisoned at the Conciergerie, also known as the antechamber to the guillotine.

DANDELION
SEED HEAD

DAME'S
ROCKET

DAPHNE
MEZEREUM

DAISY

DANDELION

Dandelion

RUSTIC ORACLE

To make a wish and blow on the feathery white seed head of a dandelion is to let your wish take flight, carried by the wind before it comes true. In French, this wildflower is known as *pissenlit*, which translates to "piss in the bed." Not only is the yellow dandelion the color of urine, but it has also been used as a natural diuretic. The flower was brought to the Americas by European settlers on the *Mayflower* as a medicinal plant and salad green.

Dandelion Seed Head
Depart

Daphne mezereum

DESIRE TO PLEASE

The daphne flower, described as donning a summer dress in the midst of winter, is noted for its early, colorful bloom. *Mezereum* is likely a derivative of the plant's Persian name *Madzaryoun*, which translates to "destroyer of life." Some birds enjoy the shrub's berries, and their droppings are an effective method of spreading the seed. The same berries, however, produce a poison that results in violent reactions in humans.

Daphne odora
Sweets to the sweet

Datura

DECEITFUL CHARMS

Also known as **Thornapple, Hell's Bells, Devil's Trumpet**. The trumpet-shaped flowers and seeds of *Datura*, which release from thorny capsules, are poisonous. All parts of this plant contain psychoactive properties resulting in delirium, hallucination, and sometimes death. In the early 1800s, a centuries-old organized gang from India known as "Thugs" were said to be responsible for approximately fifty thousand murders in one year. They used *Datura* to stupefy victims of violent acts of robbery and strangulation. The English word *thug* originates from the Hindi word meaning "swindler." According to some researchers, the murderous narrative needs reassessment and was in fact an exaggeration, if not a product of the British colonial imagination.

Violet *Datura*
Ecclesiastical

White *Datura*
Science

Daylily

COQUETRY

Also known as **Belle du Jour**. The daylily blooms during the day and coyly retracts as evening falls. Daylilies are used in Chinese, Japanese, Thai, and Vietnamese cuisine. The dried buds, known as "golden needles," are added to recipes to symbolize wealth during celebrations for the Chinese lunar new year.

DELPHINIUM

Delphinium

LEVITY

Derived from the Greek word for "dolphin," this flower's buds slightly resemble the sleek sea creature. Delphiniums are also known as **larkspur**; a seedpod from this flower is said to look like the foot of a lark. The joyful songbird is beloved for its sweet and uplifting tune.

Pink Delphinium
Fickleness

Purple Delphinium
Haughtiness

DATURA

DAYLILY

Dittany of Crete

BIRTH

Dittany of Crete is a shrubby plant with soft, velvety leaves covered in a pale fuzz and accented by pink-and-purple blooms, native to the mountaintops of the Greek island of Crete. Roman naturalist Pliny the Elder described use of this plant as an effective way to ease childbirth, even in cases where the baby was breech. The flower's name means "love" in Cretan dialect, and many ardent lovers hike along the mountains and gorges of the island to procure some. Over the centuries, many men have died in the attempt to fetch bunches of these blooms for their paramours.

DITTANY OF CRETE

Dogbane

FALSEHOOD

The term *bane* was originally used to refer to something that caused death. When added to plant names, it revealed a plant's particular poisonous nature. Dogbane was known to kill or repel canines.

DOGWOOD

DOGBANE

DRAGONWORT

Dogwood

DURABILITY

Chewing on sticks as a method of oral hygiene has a long history, tracing back as far as 3500 BCE in Babylonia. This technique has long been used by people across Asia, Africa, and the Americas. Until the late eighteenth century, Europeans simply wiped their teeth with salted rags. Early American colonists caught on to the Indigenous ways and used frayed dogwood twigs as toothbrushes. Bark would be stripped from young twigs and a good chew would spread the tip of the twig into a fibrous brush. According to *Gunn's Domestic Medicine* (1831), this method was superior to the newfangled toothbrushes, which were made of hog bristles.

Dragonwort

HORROR

The putrid smell of dragonwort is reminiscent of rotting meat. Flies attracted to this stink are its pollinators. The flower can increase its own temperature up to 64.4°F (18°C), providing a comfortable environment for insects to do their business.

EBONY

ELDER

ELM

E

Ebony

BLACKNESS

Some of the finest ebony wood comes from Sri Lanka. Peel back the jet-black bark to find pure white wood—until you get to the heart. The black heartwood is considered the best part of the tree because of its durability, hardness, and the ability to polish up nicely. The ancient kings of India had their scepters carved from this wood. Today, ebony is used to make cabinetry, knife handles, and piano keys.

Elder

ZEALOUSNESS

High in vitamin C, elderflowers and their berries are used in cuisines and herbal remedies around the world. According to European folklore, if you sit under an elder bush on a midsummer night, you are likely to receive a visit from fairies and elves. The fragrance emits a mild sedative; it is suspected that the folktales originated from some drugged-out dreams.

Elm

DIGNITY

The elm is a proud tree, emblematic of numerous revolutions. After the Parliamentarians claimed victory over the monarchists in England's Glorious Revolution of 1688, the Dutch elm hybrid gained popularity as a political statement of enthusiasm for the new order. In the following century, American colonists held their first resistance meetings in front of a particular white elm in Boston. Since the British knew the tree to be a symbol of rebellion, they chopped it down in 1775. The Americans responded by sewing "Liberty Elm" badges to their revolutionary flags and organizing widespread plantings of their new symbol—the Liberty Elm.

American Elm
Patriotism

Enchanter's Nightshade

SORCERY

Despite its name, the enchanter's nightshade is an herbaceous plant in the evening primrose—not nightshade—family. These little white florets grow on a slender stem and thrive in dark, damp woodlands. The Latin name *Circaea canadensis* comes from the Greek enchantress and goddess of magic, Circe, who was revered for her extensive knowledge of herbs. She lived in a wooded area on the island of Aeaea. In Homer's epic the *Odyssey*, she notoriously cast a spell transforming Odysseus's crew into swine.

Eupatorium

DELAY

Clusters of tiny pink or white flowers emerge above the foliage, enticing butterflies to rest on this ornamental plant. Native Americans used this flower as an herbal medication for colds and flus. The common name **boneset** is a direct reference to its use as a treatment for the tropical dengue fever. The illness was also called "break-bone fever" due to the severe pain experienced in muscles, joints, and bones.

EUPATORIUM

EVENING PRIMROSE

ENCHANTER'S NIGHTSHADE

EVERLASTING PEA

Evening Primrose

INCONSTANCY

Also known as **Suncup, Sundrop**. The evening primrose is named to reflect the time of day it blooms. The flowers unfurl quickly, sometimes opening in less than one minute. The seed oil has been used as an herbal remedy for a variety of ailments including eczema, arthritis, migraines, PMS, and hot flashes associated with menopause.

Everlasting Pea

LASTING PLEASURE; AN APPOINTED MEETING

A cousin of the sweet pea, the everlasting pea is a perennial that supports many small creatures. Tiger moth caterpillars as well as other herbivores consume the leaves of this straggly vine. Butterflies enjoy the nectar of these flowers, although it is actually the bumblebee that pollinates this scentless bloom.

F

Fennel

STRENGTH

With a delicious aroma and the flavor of anise, fennel was a popular vegetable in ancient Greece. Consuming it was believed to help build strength while remaining thin. The Greeks named the plant "marathon," taken from *maraino*, meaning "to grow thin." The city of Marathon was named after the wild, flowering fennel that grew all over the region. When the Athenians defeated the Persians in a legendary battle in Marathon, a Greek herald was tasked to announce the victory. He ran 26.22 miles from Marathon to Athens without a break. The endurance race, popularized by the Olympics, is still measured at that distance. During the Roman era, victors in competitive games of sport were crowned with wreaths of fennel.

Fern

SINCERITY

Ferns of all varieties are valued as sacred plants by Celtic and Germanic cultures. In ancient times, some correctly thought the fern had no seeds; others thought the seeds were invisible. Druids believed that if you were to behold the fern seed, you would be granted powers of invisibility. This legend is referenced in Shakespeare's *Henry IV*: "We steal as in a castle, cocksure: we have the receipt of fern-seed, we walk invisible."

Flowering Fern
Reverie

Maidenhair Fern
Discretion

100

FLOWERS AND THEIR MEANINGS \

FENNEL

FERN

Fever Root

DELAY

Also known as **Minnieroot, Sheep Potato**. Fever root is a favorite plant of children, not for its violet funnel-shaped flowers but for its unusual seeds. When the dried pods are exposed to water (or rubbed with a child's spit), each long, thin pod suddenly pops, almost like a little jumping grasshopper. Children toss the wet seedpods at unaware passersby, startling their victims with an explosion of tiny seeds.

Fig Blossom

PROLIFIC

Also known as **Ficus**. One of the first plants to be domesticated was the fig tree. Figs are sacred to many religious groups around the world. The Buddha achieved enlightenment while sitting under the *Ficus religiosa*, also known as the Bodhi tree. The Mahabodhi Temple—a preserved World Heritage Site and popular pilgrimage destination in Bihar, India—was built on that very spot. Tourists can visit a tree that is descended from the original.

FEVER ROOT

FIR

FIREWEED

FIG BLOSSOM

Fir

ELEVATION

The Christmas tree was popularized in 1848 when an illustration of Queen Victoria, Prince Albert, and their children circulated around the world. The family was pictured gathered around a fir tree decorated with lit candles and colorful paper nets suspending golden apples and nuts in the evergreen branches. The German prince Albert grew up with Christmas trees, which have been a traditional form of holiday decor since the eighteenth century. The tradition became fashionable in England and North America, and though some cultures still viewed gathering around a tree as a pagan ritual, it became an important part of middle-class Christian families' celebrations.

Fireweed

CELIBACY

Also known as **Rosebay Willowherb**. This flower is especially abundant in recently scorched fields or cleared forests. Fireweed is often used as a rehabilitating plant to help the recovery of disturbed land. The flowers grow in these open areas as long as they have access to full sunlight. Eventually, new trees and brush grow, repopulating the once-devastated land. In the event of another disturbance, the dormant fireweed seeds will germinate and grow once again.

Flax

I FEEL YOUR KINDNESS

Cultivated for its edible seeds, linseed oil, and linen cloth, it is not surprising that the Latin name for flax is *usitatissimum*, which means "most useful." Evidence of spun and dyed flax fibers dates back thirty thousand years to the Upper Paleolithic era. In ancient Egypt, priests wore only linen and the pretty flowering plant was celebrated in wall paintings inside tombs.

Dried Flax
Utility

Forget-Me-Not

FORGET ME NOT

German legend tells of a knight attempting to procure a sprig of flowers for his betrothed along the Danube River. When the knight falls in the water and is carried away by the current, he tosses the flowers to his love on shore, calling out, *"Vergiss mich nicht!,"* or "Do not forget me!" This plant's tiny seedpods cling to passersby. Once attached to animals' fur or to pant legs, they will join travelers to their next destination.

FLAX

FRANKINCENSE

FORGET-ME-NOT

FOXGLOVE

Foxglove

A WISH

Despite its notorious toxicity, this flower has long been known for its medicinal properties. It is suspected that Van Gogh took foxglove extract during his yellow period to control epileptic seizures. Side effects include blurred vision (with a yellow tinge) and the appearance of halos emanating from points of light. Perhaps most evident in *Starry Night*, these visual distortions perfectly describe the painter's iconic work. Van Gogh also painted two portraits of his doctor, Paul Gachet. Both feature a stem of foxglove.

Frankincense

THE INCENSE OF A FAITHFUL HEART

The dried sap of *Boswellia* trees—frankincense—is burned as incense in Catholic masses as well as Arabic weddings and birth ceremonies. The Old French phrase *franc encens*, meaning "high-quality incense," is the original source of the English name. Frankincense was believed to ward off evil spirits and snakes and was considered as precious as gold. It quickly became the most lucrative commodity in the world, with much of the trade protected by fortresses in Oman in a place now dubbed the Land of Frankincense.

Fraxinella

FIRE

Also known as **Dittany**. Fraxinella, native to the Middle East, emits a flammable oil that is capable of spontaneous combustion on a hot day. It is suspected that the biblical image of Moses's burning bush was a flowering fraxinella plant on fire.

White Fraxinella
Passion

French Honeysuckle

RUSTIC BEAUTY

Botanically unrelated to the honeysuckle family, these crimson blooms feature up to thirty-five florets per head. Honeybees are so fond of the flower's nectar that some beekeepers move their hives to where French honeysuckle grows wild to cultivate this specific, delicious honey.

Fritillaria, Checkered

PERSECUTION

Fritillaria are named after a Roman dice cup used to prevent cheating in ancient games. The patterned bell-shaped blooms are sometimes called **mission bells** in North America. The Victorian meaning of persecution attributed to this flower is in honor of Noël Capperon, the French apothecary credited with discovering this flower. He was later murdered during the St. Bartholomew's Day massacre.

FUCHSIA

FRENCH HONEYSUCKLE

FUMITORY

SCARLET
FUCHSIA

FRAXINELLA

FRITILLARIA,
CHECKERED

FULLER'S
TEASEL

Fuchsia

TH'AMBITION IN MY LOVE THUS
PLAGUES ITSELF

Also known as **Lady's Ear Drops**. This flower belongs to the realm of fairies. Pluck all but two stamens and it even looks like a dancing sprite. This species is primarily native to Central and South America. The fuchsia tree *kōtukutuku* in New Zealand produces a blue pollen, which is used as makeup by the Māori people. This flower comes in a variety of pink colors, but the bright dark pink with blue undertones is where the color fuchsia got its name.

Scarlet Fuchsia
Taste

Fuller's Teasel

MISANTHROPY

Clothiers and fullers (workers who cleanse wool) would raise the nap of their woolen clothes with the long and sharp thorns of this sturdy egg-shaped flower head. Once the bursts of tiny lavender blooms fall away, the hooked spiny bracts remain, perfectly sized to be used as a handheld tool.

Fumitory

SPLEEN

Also known as **Fumewort**. Thought to resemble a puff of smoke piping up from the ground, this plant was known in the thirteenth century as *firmus terrae*, or "smoke of the earth." The name reflects the teary reaction that occurs when one touches their eye after handling the flower. Some species are used in herbal medicine; it was once believed that an infusion made from the pungent foliage could erase freckles.

107 \ FLOWERS AND THEIR MEANINGS

GARDEN
MYRRH

GARDENIA

GALIUM

GALEGA

G

Galega

REASON

Also known as **Goat's Rue, Professor-Weed**. Medieval Europeans believed this flowering purple herb possessed many medicinal properties. An herbal tonic was used to treat the bubonic plague. It was also believed to promote lactation in mammalian mothers and was used to increase the milk supply in goats, cows, and humans.

Galium

PATIENCE

Also known as **Lady's Bedstraw**. In the Middle Ages, dried *Galium* was collected for stuffing mattresses. This occurred throughout Europe—even ladies of rank enjoyed this bedding. The plant is a flea repellent but could not keep moths away. Many species of Lepidoptera feed on *Galium*, including the elephant hawk, flame shoulder, and autumnal rustic moths.

Garden Myrrh

GLADNESS

When crushed, garden myrrh releases a strong fragrance similar to anise. The fern-like foliage is sometimes used to add flavor to the alcoholic spirit aquavit. The dried leaves and seeds can be used as a sugar substitute.

Gardenia

TRANSPORT OF JOY

Also known as **Cape Jasmine**. At the 1939 Academy Awards, Hattie McDaniel wore gardenias in her hair when she accepted an Oscar for her performance in *Gone with the Wind*. McDaniel was the first African American to win an Oscar. In 2010, Mo'Nique wore a similar floral hairpiece as a tribute to McDaniel when she won an Oscar for her performance in *Precious*.

Gentian

I LOVE YOU BEST WHEN YOU ARE SAD

This autumnal flower is known in Japan as *rindou.* The characters that spell out this word translate roughly as "dragon liver." The Japanese symbolism is "strong sense of justice" and "accurate." Yellow gentian is a key ingredient in many drinks, including Angostura bitters, Aperol, and Moxie soda. Most often, this flower is a deep purple-blue. In the nineteenth century, advertisements for home goods, clothing, and paints started to promote the color gentian blue.

Yellow Gentian
Ingratitude

GENTIAN

Geranium

GENTILITY

Lightly pinch the fuzzy leaves of a scented geranium and a unique fragrance will be released from the flower's glandular hairs. Muslim legend says that the prophet Muhammad imbued the plant with perfume after drying his shirt on its humble blossoms. During the Elizabethan era, a pale chalky face contrasted with red lips—which was popularized by the queen herself—was considered stylish. This lipstick was produced with beeswax mixed with dried flowers, such as geranium or rose.

Apple-Scented Geranium
Present preference

Cranesbill Geranium
Envy

Fish Geranium
Disappointed expectation

Ivy Geranium
Your hand for the next dance

Lemon-Scented Geranium
Unexpected meeting

Nutmeg-Scented Geranium
Expected meeting

Oak-Leaved Geranium
True friendship

Pencil-Leaf Geranium
Ingenuity

Rose-Scented Geranium
Preference

Sad Geranium
Melancholy spirit

Scarlet Geranium
Stupidity

GERANIUM

Gladiolus

READY ARMED

Named from the Latin word meaning "little sword," this flower of the gladiators is said to pierce the heart with love. Originating from South Africa, the flowers, which grow in a multitude of hues, bloom from spiky buds that line up in a row along the stalk. The long leaves resembling blades create a sheath. In the seventeenth century, there were seven species. Since then, more than ten thousand varieties of *Gladiolus* hybrids have been cultivated.

Glasswort

PRETENSION

It is rumored that there was no English name for this flower until the sixteenth century, when visiting glassmakers from Italy pointed out the usefulness of this plant. The ashes of glasswort could be used to make soda-based glass. When the plant is burned to ash, any sodium that had been absorbed from salt water transforms into useful sodium carbonate, which is a critical component of glassmaking.

Goldenrod

ENCOURAGEMENT

Goldenrod is a valued garden flower in England but is considered a weed in America. During World War II, the botanist and inventor George Washington Carver, who maintained a fruitful correspondence with Henry Ford, was asked by Ford to help invent a synthetic rubber. In 1942, after experimenting with several plants, Carver developed a method to create synthetic rubber from the flowering goldenrod plant.

GOLDENROD

GLADIOLUS

GOOSEBERRY

GOOD-KING-HENRY

*GOLDILOCKS
ASTER*

Goldilocks Aster

TARDINESS

The moniker Goldilocks has been affectionately given to various yellow flowering plants, especially those with bush-like button heads—like this relative of the daisy and the dandelion. This particular species of flaxen blooms is often found growing in gravelly areas or on limestone outcrops.

Good-King-Henry

GOODNESS

Often grown in English cottage and vegetable gardens, young Good-King-Henry shoots were enjoyed as ***poor man's asparagus***. The flowers were sautéed in butter and eaten like broccoli, and the succulent leaves were prepared like spinach.

Gooseberry

ANTICIPATION

When asked where babies come from, British children were sometimes told to look under a gooseberry bush. As a cheeky reference to this folk tale, nineteenth-century Brits called pubic hair "gooseberry bush."

GLASSWORT

Gourd Blossom

BULK

Fruits of the gourd family include pumpkins, calabash, zucchini, and many varieties of melons and squash. When the seeds inside a gourd are left to dry, the fruit transforms into a rattle. Some cultures used gourds as percussion instruments, believing the sound frightened away evil spirits. Carved gourds have been used to make musical instruments, dishware, tools, and toys for centuries.

Grass

SUBMISSION

See page 116.
According to Irish myth, a patch of cursed grass is called "hungry grass." Any person who walks across one of these hexed plots is doomed forever to be insatiably hungry. Lore suggests that fairies plant this grass, but many suspect that the concept for hungry grass was formed during the Great Famine of the 1840s, when many were suffering from intense hunger pangs.

Canary Grass
Perseverance

Rye Grass
Changeable disposition

Vernal Grass
Poor but happy

GRASS

GROUND LAUREL

Greater Celandine

FIRST SIGH OF LOVE

Antoine Bret, a French poet and playwright from the eighteenth century, once wrote, "The first sigh of love is the last of wisdom." Ants carry these seeds to their nests, effectively helping spread the flower. Greater celandine has been used for a variety of medicinal purposes, including soothing dyspepsia, gout, and genital warts.

Ground Laurel

PERSEVERANCE

Also known as **Trailing Arbutus, Mayflower**. Ground laurel holds deep importance for the Bodéwadmi (Potawatomi) people of North America. Believed to hold a direct connection to the tribe's divinity, it is regarded as their tribal flower. The low-spreading shrub, with its fragrant white flowers, is the official floral emblem of both Massachusetts and Nova Scotia. Picking ground laurel in either place is illegal.

GREATER CELANDINE

GOURD BLOSSOM

115

Grass

SUBMISSION

See page 114

The modern lawn is typically recognized as a rectangular stretch of neatly mowed green grass. Historically, a swath of land that held no purpose other than as an expanse of space was a blatant display of wealth. During the Renaissance, an English or French lawn was typically cultivated with plants like chamomile and thyme as opposed to grass, and grazing cattle became a natural method of lawn maintenance.

The carefully shorn, manicured lawns we know today were introduced in the seventeenth century. Attainable only to the extremely wealthy, not only did this empty landscape show off an excess of property, but it also necessitated a lot of human labor to carefully hand-snip or scythe it.

The tall and billowy grasses native to North America include switchgrass, bluestem, and buffalo grass, which can grow higher than nine feet tall. Colonists brought seeds to re-create the rolling landscapes and grazing pastures of Europe. The types of grass that have become so pervasive across the United States, such as Kentucky bluegrass and Bermuda grass, are not native species. They quickly and aggressively spread across the continent.

In the nineteenth century, famed landscape architect Frederick Law Olmsted incorporated carefully planned meadows into his beloved city parks. He is most known for masterpieces such as Central Park in New York City as well as parks in Boston, Montreal, and other major metropolitan areas. He also designed residential suburbs where each home could support a lawn if the owner chose to grow one. In the twentieth century, Levittown in Long Island became the first American suburb to provide lawns—installed from the get-go—when the residents took possession of their new homes.

H

Hackberry

CONCEIT

Also known as **Nettle Tree, Lote Tree**. Not to be confused with the painful stinging nettle, this deciduous tree's fruit and leaves are used in the cuisine of many American Indigenous cultures, including the Dakota and Chatiks si chatiks (Pawnee). In the *Odyssey*, Homer tells of a land of lotus-eaters. Some scholars believe that the lotus in this story was the fruit of the nettle tree. Competing theories suggest the jujube and the blue water lily, as the Greek word *lôtos* was used somewhat indiscriminately to describe a wide variety of unrelated plants.

Hand Flower

WARNING

Also known as **Devil's Hand Tree, Monkey's Hand Flower**. The hand flower tree is aptly named, as its blooms look like open palms with fingers outstretched. The Aztecs revered the tree and called the plant *mācpalxōchitl*, or palm flower, in their native Nahuatl. They used an herbal hand flower concoction as a medicinal treatment for heart problems and abdominal pain.

Harebell

GRIEF

Also known as **Witches' Thimble, Nun of the Fields, Bluebell of Scotland**. The lovely nodding blue bells of this flower grow in Scottish fields where rabbits roam. According to local superstition, upon seeing a patch of harebell, passersby should proceed cautiously—a witch could transform herself into a hare and be hidden among the blooms. It was believed that wearing a sprig of harebell compelled its wearer to tell the complete truth in all matters.

Hawkweed

QUICK-SIGHTEDNESS

Often confused with dandelions, this weedy flower was once linked to sharp eyesight. In England and throughout Europe, it was believed that hawks dropped sap from this yellow flower into the eyes of their chicks to improve their vision. When falconry was common, the plant was fed to birds with this purpose in mind. In the seventeenth century, herbalist Nicholas Culpeper suggested an application of hawkweed and breast milk to cure all defects of the human eye.

HAWKWEED

HACKBERRY

HAREBELL

HAND FLOWER

Hawthorn

HOPE

Also known as **Thorn Apple, May Tree**. Across Scotland and Ireland, hawthorn trees are often found next to sacred springs or wells. These ancient Celtic sites, known as clootie wells, are used for healing rituals. For those seeking healing, a strip of cloth is dipped into the holy waters and tied onto the nearby tree's branches before a hopeful prayer is spoken into the well. Pagans who made pilgrimages to clootie wells worshipped various nature spirits and goddesses. Christians call on modern-day saints.

Hazel

RECONCILIATION

Also known as **Filbert**. The bounty offered by this shrubby tree is the delicious hazelnut. Rods from the hazel tree are also used by diviners to detect underground sources of water. A forked stick, held loosely with both hands, allegedly bends toward water. Some say a rod of hazel wood can also detect precious metals, hidden treasures, and fugitive assassins. Although this technique—called dowsing—is considered pseudoscience, there are still some U.K. and U.S. farmers who practice this form of divination.

HELENIUM

HEATHER

HAZEL

HELIOTROPE

HAWTHORN

Heather

SOLITUDE

Also known as **Erica**. Heather flourishes in the acidic soil and dreary conditions found in the Scottish Highlands. Folktales from that region claim the pink and red varieties grow from land where blood was once shed. In 1884, after the language of flowers craze had waned, Queen Victoria spread the notion that the less common white heather was an emblem of good luck.

Helenium

TEARS

Also known as *Sneezeweed*. The Menominee people of Wisconsin named this flower *aiatci'a ni'tcîkûn*, meaning "sneezing spasmodically." Long ago, dried helenium used to be made into snuff. A sniff of the stuff would trigger sneezing, believed to expel evil spirits from the body.

Heliotrope

DEVOTION

In Greek mythology, grief-stricken Clytie was abandoned by Helios, the god and personification of the sun. She camped out by a river without any food for nine sleepless days to simply watch Helios's chariot rise and set. The gods transformed the water nymph into a flower, calling it a heliotrope, meaning "sun turn." Sunflowers are often mistaken as heliotropic, but once they are in full bloom, sunflowers face east all day. The purple heliotrope flower, on the other hand, never stops tracking the sun.

121

FLOWERS AND THEIR MEANINGS

Hellebore

SCANDAL

Also known as **Christmas Rose**. Hellebore was used by the Greeks to taint the water supply of the city of Kirrha in 585 BCE during the First Sacred War. The victims, taken by serious bouts of diarrhea, were unable to defend themselves from siege. Kirrha was captured and destroyed.

Hemlock

YOU WILL CAUSE MY DEATH

In ancient Greece, hemlock was often used to poison and kill criminals. When Socrates was convicted of corrupting the youth of Athens in 339 BCE, he was sentenced to drink a poisonous infusion of hemlock. His student Plato witnessed his death and provided a descriptive account of the ordeal. The crushed leaves of this plant smell like parsnips or mice.

Henbane

IMPERFECTION

A juice made from henbane, mandrake, and poppy was used as an anesthetic from ancient Roman times until the nineteenth century, when chloroform was invented. The solution was often dried for storage and reconstituted with water when needed. The potion was unreliable and risky, and patients sometimes felt everything during surgery or died. Medieval necromancers used this herb in rituals to commune with the dead.

HOLLY

HEMLOCK

HEPATICA

HENBANE

HELLEBORE

HIBISCUS

Hepatica

CONFIDENCE

Also known as **Liverwort**. These poised flowers proudly radiate beautiful hues of blue and purple. Named after the Greek word for liver, *Hepatica* bears three-lobed leaves that look like the organ and was believed to be a remedy for medical issues involving the liver. The leaves and flowers have been used as a diuretic, although the plant is poisonous when consumed in large amounts.

Hibiscus

DELICATE BEAUTY

A woman in Hawaii or Tahiti can communicate her relationship status by wearing a hibiscus flower in her hair. Tucked behind the right ear, she broadcasts that she is single and looking for a mate. Worn on the left side, she confirms that she is a married woman. The Chinese name for this flower translates as "husband appearing."

Holly

FORESIGHT

Druids wore sprigs of holly in their hair, believing the plant could protect against evil. During Saturnalia, the Roman holiday that eventually transformed into Christmas, boughs of the tree were popular gifts to exchange among friends. During the twelve days of Christmas, celebrated in Tudor England, holly and other winter greenery were brought inside to decorate for the holiday. Many households tied garlands around the home's spinning wheel, rendering it inoperative until the epic holiday revelry had concluded.

Hollyhock

FECUNDITY

Occasionally referred to as **outhouse flowers**, tall and lovely hollyhocks were often planted to disguise unsightly outhouses. Ranging in color from pink, red, and purple to yellow, blue, and black, these vertical stalks are covered in colorful blooms from top to bottom, leaving very little bare stem.

White Hollyhock
Female ambition

Dark-Colored Hollyhock
Ambition

Honey Flower

LOVE SWEET AND SECRET

Honey flower is known in its native South Africa as *kruidjie-roer-my-nie* (Afrikaans for "herb-touch-me-not") because of the distinct aroma released when the leaves are pinched. Some describe a pungent stink; others compare the smell to peanut butter or honey. The cup-shaped flowers fill up and sometimes overflow with black nectar, which pollinating birds enjoy.

HONEYSUCKLE

HOPS

HOLLYHOCK

HONEY FLOWER

Honeysuckle

BONDS OF LOVE

Tough honeysuckle vines have long been used to produce strong rope. In the early Bronze Age, honeysuckle ropes were used to arrange the tree stumps that make up the prehistoric monument Seahenge. Anthropologists believe the circle of fifty-five upturned split oak stumps, located on the beach of Norfolk, England, was used for ritual purposes.

Coral Honeysuckle
The color of my fate

Variegated-Leaf Honeysuckle
Fraternal love

Hops

INJUSTICE

The flowers of the hop plant, commonly used as a stability and flavoring agent in beer, grow in a twisting, clockwise direction. The climbing tendrils are trained to grow up trellises or may scrabble up the sides of buildings. Try to redirect the vines and they will correct course, returning to their comfortable clockwise pattern. Hops were originally added to beer as an antibacterial preservative. Beer produced for transport to India was made with massive amounts of hops so the liquid would last for the long journey. This particular beer became known as India pale ale.

Hornbeam

ORNAMENT

Used to create living archways, hornbeam was a popular ornamental feature of large gardens. Also known as **ironwood**, the hard timber from a hornbeam tree was often used to make durable objects, such as cutting boards, tool handles, wheels, and gear pegs for simple machines.

Horse Chestnut

LUXURY

When this tree is in full bloom, the visual effect is reminiscent of an old-fashioned chandelier with dozens of upright candles sprouting from the fixture's arms. Anne Frank wrote longingly in her diary about the horse chestnut viewable from her attic window. That particular tree was one of the oldest chestnut trees in Amsterdam and became a symbol of freedom for the Jewish teenager while she hid from the Nazis for more than two years. Although an intense storm knocked it down in 2010, many saplings propagated from that tree have been planted around the world.

Houseleek

DOMESTIC INDUSTRY

Also known as **Welcome-home-husband-though-never-so-drunk**. Charlemagne, first emperor of the Holy Roman Empire, made it mandatory for every landlord to plant one houseleek on the roof of every dwelling to protect it against fire, lightning, witches, and pestilence. This superstition was adopted in various parts of medieval Europe, and to this day there is evidence of Welsh people keeping this tradition alive. The hardy succulent is admired for its ability to retain life even on hot rooftops.

HORNBEAM

HOUSELEEK

HOYA

HORSE CHESTNUT

HYACINTH

Hoya

SCULPTURE

Also known as **Waxplant**. The hoya plant's buds grow in tightly packed, globular clusters of up to forty star-shaped flowers. Each bud appears to be perfectly sculpted from porcelain or wax. Recent studies suggest that the hoya can remove pollutants from indoor environments.

Hyacinth

PLAY

Greek mythology tells of Hyacinthus, a beautiful Spartan prince, playing a game of quoits with his lover, Apollo. Out of jealousy, one of the prince's many admirers disrupted the game by using the wind to redirect the path of a heavy horseshoe-like ring, striking Hyacinthus dead. A grief-stricken Apollo transformed the prince's blood into the flower hyacinth.

Blue Hyacinth
Constancy

Feathered Hyacinth
Excess of beauty hath bewitched me

Purple Hyacinth
I am sorry

White Hyacinth
Unobtrusive loveliness

Yellow Hyacinth
The heart demands more incense than flattery

Hydrangea

BOASTER

Also known as **Hortensia**. The Bunkyō
Hydrangea Festival—one of the many
hydrangea festivals in Japan—is held every
summer at Tokyo's Hakusan Shrine when
hydrangeas are in full bloom. For some
unknown reason, the shrine has been
associated with dental care since the Edo
period (between 1603 and 1867). Visitors
are given a toothbrush while viewing the
beautiful, fluffy flowers.

Hyssop

CLEANLINESS

There are several mentions of hyssop in
the Bible, such as in Psalm 51:7: "Purge
me with hyssop, and I shall be clean." In
the story of Passover, which appears in
the book of Exodus, Jews used hyssop to
splash the blood of the sacrificial lamb on
doorposts as a form of protection from
the angel of death. Upon seeing the door
smeared with blood, the angel would know
to "pass over" certain houses, sparing its
Jewish inhabitants from sickness or death.

HYDRANGEA

HYSSOP

IMPATIENS

ICE PLANT

I

Ice Plant

YOUR LOOKS FREEZE ME

In sunlight, ice plants sparkle as if frozen and covered in ice crystals. Tiny transparent bladder cells on the outermost layer of the plant that reserve water seem to glisten in the sunlight. Some ice plant species bear edible fruit and leaves, which are available in grocery stores throughout Japan.

Impatiens

IMPATIENCE

Also known as **Balsam**. With the slightest touch, a ripe balsam capsule's seeds will dart out and scatter at a distance. In Korea, the flower was often planted around the home to ward off evil spirits and disease. The flowers are also used in a Korean cosmetic to color fingernails; a mixture of the flower and alum creates a semipermanent dye. Korean superstition states that if a trace of the color remains by the time of the first snowfall, wearers will marry their true love.

Red Impatiens
Touch me not

Indian Plum

PRIVATION

Also known as **Osoberry, Skunkbush**. The leaves of the Indian plum have a scent comparable to cucumbers, but the white blossoms notoriously smell like cat urine. Although the wood of this early-blooming shrub is quite strong, the stems rarely grow beyond two inches in diameter, limiting how the wood can be used. The sturdy, straight shoots have been used to make arrows, knitting needles, and combs.

Iris

MESSAGE

Named after the Greek goddess of rainbows, Iris, this vibrant, multicolored flower represents the bright days of spring. Iris, the swift messenger to the gods, was known to bring good news. One of her sacred duties was to guide the souls of good women to their final resting place in the Elysian Fields, which led to the Greek tradition of planting a purple iris near a woman's grave. It was also believed that consuming an iris would extend one's longevity.

Flame Iris
Flame

IRIS

INDIAN PLUM

Ivy

MARRIAGE

Ivy won't accept every support it is offered,
but once this vine with heart-shaped
leaves clings to a surface, it is forever. If
the attachment is broken, the ivy will die. A
symbol of endless unity, it is Greek tradition
to gift a bride and groom two sprigs of
this plant.

Ivy sprig with tendrils
Assiduous to please

IVY

J

Jacob's-Ladder

COME DOWN

Also known as **Greek Valerian**. In the Bible, Jacob dreams of a ladder that leads straight to heaven. The plant's evenly stacked leaves resemble the rungs of a ladder. Jacob's-ladder was used as an herbal remedy in ancient Greece for dysentery, animal bites, and toothaches. In the nineteenth century, the hardy flowering plant was sold in pharmacies as an antisyphilitic treatment.

Jasmine

AMIABILITY

Jasmine is one of the most popular flowers in the world, second only to the rose. The name is a derivative of the Persian *yasmin*, meaning "gift from God." It is most cherished for its intoxicating perfume. In Tunisia, a small bundle of jasmine is known as *machmoum*. Men tuck the fragrant bouquet behind a particular ear to indicate their relationship status.

Indian Jasmine
I attach myself to you

Spanish Jasmine
Sensuality

Yellow Jasmine
First language of love

JACOB'S-LADDER

JASMINE

Judas

BETRAYAL

This species is named after the traitorous disciple of Jesus, who supposedly hanged himself from this deciduous tree, causing its abundant white flowers to turn red. Because of this tale, some people consider the species to be satanic. Other sources believe the original name for the tree was a misunderstanding of the French *arbre de Judée*, or "tree of Judea," in reference to the tree's location in the Roman province of Judca (present-day Palestine).

Juniper

PROTECTION

Long used as a healing and purifying botanical, juniper has been found to have antiseptic and antifungal properties. Oil harvested from this resinous conifer was used to prevent infection during the Spanish flu pandemic of 1918. Hospitals sprayed a vaporized oil to curb the spread of airborne particles.

Justicia

PERFECTION OF FEMALE LOVELINESS

The *Justicia* plant features densely packed plumes of showy flowers that appear in a variety of colors, including pinks and corals. The curved bracts, reminiscent of a certain sea creature, earned this tropical plant the name **Mexican shrimp plant**. The phytochemical components found in the essential oils of this plant are being studied for potential antitumor and antiviral properties.

JUNIPER

JUSTICIA

JUDAS

KENNEDIA

KNOTGRASS

K

Kennedia

MENTAL BEAUTY

Kennedias grow as scrambling ground cover, dotted with scarlet pea flowers, each with a touch of yellow. The tough stems of this plant were once used as string by the Indigenous people of Australia. The colloquial name **running postman** is a reference to the bright red jackets worn by Australian postal workers during the nineteenth century. Indigenous elder Auntie Wendall Pitchford recently proposed renaming the bloom "running warrior" in honor of the Tasmanian lives lost during the colonial massacre known as the Australian Frontier Wars.

Knotgrass

RESTORATION

Also known as **Polygonum**, *Pigweed*. The white or pink flowers of knotgrass are often spotted along roadsides throughout Britain. Shakespeare mentions the plant in *A Midsummer Night's Dream*. Lysander says to Hermia, "Get you gone, you dwarf, / You minimus of hindering knotgrass made, / You bead, you acorn!" At the time, a decoction of this plant was believed to stunt the growth of children. So "knotgrass made" was an insulting way to comment on a person's diminutive size.

139

L

Laburnum

PENSIVE BEAUTY

Also known as **Golden Rain**. Pendulous clusters of sweetly fragrant, yellow flowers hang from the laburnum tree. The wood used to be a popular choice to make musical wind instruments. All parts of this tree are considered poisonous, resulting in headaches, vomiting, convulsions, and death.

Lantana

RIGOR

Some types of birds, such as the black-throated weaver and the streaked weaver, use fragrant and colorful lantana flowers to decorate their nests. A uniquely and well-decorated nest is considered a signal of mate-worthiness to visiting female birds.

LEAVES, DEAD

Larch

AUDACITY

Among the bright green needles of the deciduous larch tree are small magenta cones that could be mistaken for flowers. As spring progresses, the cones slowly turn brown, and in autumn the needles turn rusty yellow before falling off. According to the homeopath Edward Bach, inventor of Bach remedy systems, larch essence eases self-doubt. A tincture of larch, brandy, and water is purported to encourage feelings of confidence.

Lavender

DISTRUST

Having been used by Romans to scent bathing and washing water, the name lavender comes from the Latin "to wash." To "lay someone out in lavender" is to prepare a corpse in their burial attire and to mask the unpleasant odors. This aromatic camouflage is why lavender was associated with distrust. Some say that Cleopatra was killed by an asp that was hiding in a bundle of lavender.

Leaves, Dead

SADNESS

"Be like the tree, and let the dead leaves drop." This famous quote from thirteenth-century Persian poet Rumi points to the transience of nature to teach us to release our past burdens.

LANTANA

LAVENDER

LABURNUM

LARCH

Lemon Balm

JOKING

Melissa officinalis, commonly known as lemon balm, has white flowers and a mild lemon scent. Considered a "gladdening herb," it is believed to ease stress, anxiety, and gassiness. Favored by beekeepers, the plant is rubbed onto hives to attract new bees. In pre-Hellenic mythology, Aphrodite's priestesses were known as Melissae, meaning "bees," and Aphrodite was their queen bee. Honey cakes shaped in feminine forms were prepared in celebration of the goddess.

Lemon Blossom

FIDELITY IN LOVE

In 1747, natural philosopher and physician James Lind conducted experiments to determine an effective treatment for scurvy. Though the dietary importance of vitamin C was not yet known, his successful experiments involved adding lemon juice to seamen's diets. Those who suffered from the condition were each given different potential cures. Those treated with spoonfuls of vinegar or a half-pint of seawater, for example, did not show sudden improvement like those given citrus. The United Kingdom's Institute of Naval Medicine's crest features a lemon tree in Lind's honor.

Citron
Ill-natured beauty

Lemon
Zest

Lemon Tree
Correspondence

LESSER CELANDINE

LEMON BLOSSOM

LICHEN

LETTUCE

LEMON BALM

Lesser Celandine

JOYS TO COME

The appearance of these flowers in early spring is a welcome sign of the warm weather to come. In C. S. Lewis's novel *The Lion, the Witch, and the Wardrobe*, when Aslan, the lion, returns, the icy winter woodland melts away, with the ground carpeted in the yellow blooms of lesser celandine.

Lettuce

COLDHEARTEDNESS

In Greek mythology, Adonis, the mortal lover of the goddess Aphrodite, died lying in a bed of lettuce. This allegorical tale may have inspired the name "dead man's food" and the belief that eating too much lettuce would cause impotence.

Lichen

SOLITUDE

Although lichen looks like a plant, it is actually a composite organism made up of algae, or cyanobacteria, and fungi. *Pseudevernia furfuracea* has been found within the layers of linen cloth wrapped around Egyptian mummies, as well as stuffed inside corpses' body cavities. It is unknown if this lichen, commonly known as **tree moss**, was used in the mummification process for its fragrance or its absorptive, antimicrobial, and preservative properties.

Lilac

FIRST EMOTIONS OF LOVE

Fragrant clusters of lilac make an appearance in the spring, connecting this queen of shrubs to beginnings, youthfulness, and new life. Scent is believed to be the sense with the strongest connection to the past, quickly triggering emotional memories. In 1865, when Walt Whitman first heard about the Lincoln assassination, he was surrounded by the perfume of nearby lilacs. His poem "When Lilacs Last in Dooryard Bloom'd" explores how, for him, the heady floral fragrance would forever be cemented with the grief of that tragedy.

Field Lilac
Humility

White Lilac
Youth

Lily

MAJESTY

See page 148.
In Western culture, the lily represents the soul of the recently departed. In the past, the flower's enchanting fragrance evoked life's force while simultaneously disguising the putrid smell of a corpse. Contemporary American funeral services have a more restrained relationship with decorative flowers, mostly due to technological advancements in mortuary science. Floral scents, such as lily, are often mixed into the embalming fluid.

Rose Lily
Rarity

Tiger Lily
Gaudiness

White Lily
Purity

LILAC

LINDEN

LILY OF THE VALLEY

LOCUST

LILY

Yellow Lily
Falsehood

Lily of the Valley

RETURN OF HAPPINESS

Iconic French fashion designer Christian Dior used this delicate flower as the emblem for his brand, stitching it inside linings and hems and wearing it on his lapel. Superstitious that it was his lucky flower, each runway show had at least one model donning a sprig. The Fête du Muguet, the lily of the valley festival, is a national holiday in France, where little bunches of the blooms are passed out for good luck. Dior faithfully gave these flowers to each of his employees every May 1.

Linden

CONJUGAL LOVE

The sturdy linden tree bears fragrant blossoms and heart-shaped leaves. There is an official town linden in the main square of most hamlets in Germany. Some of these trees have stood as a village meeting place for more than a thousand years. The American cousin to this tree is the basswood.

Locust

AFFECTION BEYOND THE GRAVE

Also known as **Carob Tree**. In the ancient Middle East marketplace, the seeds of the locust tree were weighed against gemstones to determine their value and size. Extracted from long, dark pods, this tree's bean-like seeds were called *carobes* or *caracts*—the origin of the jewelers' term of measurement, "carat." A typical carob seed weighs approximately 0.20 grams, which is the exact weight of a gemologist's carat.

London Pride

FRIVOLITY

Also known as **St. Patrick's Cabbage, Look Up and Kiss Me, Prattling Parnell**. According to *The Language of Flowers*, written by Frederic Shoberl in 1834, no other flower compares to nature's delicately painted pale petals of London pride. As an emblem of frivolity, Shoberl warns that the pretty bloom's inclusion in a gifted nosegay might be considered an insult to a dedicated lover.

Loosestrife

RETRIBUTION

Europeans brought this beloved garden flower to the Americas, where it quickly became an aggressively invasive plant. It is considered a noxious weed in several states. The plant can expel up to 2.5 million seeds annually, clogging wetlands and choking out other species, completely altering an ecosystem. Some call it a **handsome rascal**.

Lotus

ELOQUENCE

The lotus is considered one of the world's most sacred flowers. Rising up out of the mud, it unfurls to reveal a pure white bloom. In Buddhist and Hindu cultures, the flower represents truth, perfection, and immortality. The lotus uniquely provides seedpods, buds, and fully bloomed flowers all at once. This characteristic embodies the concept of the past, present, and future coexisting.

Lotus Leaf
Recantation

LONDON PRIDE

LUPINE

LOOSESTRIFE

LUCERNE

LOTUS

Lucerne

LIFE

Lucerne has long been cultivated as hearty sustenance for livestock and as a sprouted salad green for humans. The common name **alfalfa** is derived from the Arabic phrase *al-fac-facah*, which translates as "father of all foods." Evidence of this plant has been found in six-thousand-year-old Persian remains.

Lupine

VORACIOUSNESS

Named from the Latin *lupīnus*, meaning "wolfish," it was believed that lupines greedily used up all the minerals in the soil where they were planted. The opposite is actually true: The flower is able to pull nitrogen from the air and generously fertilize the soil for other plants' use.

Rose Lupine
Imagination

Wild Blue Lupine
Her smile, the soul of witchery

Lily

MAJESTY

See page 144

In Chinese culture, the lily is a popular gifting flower. One of the longest-cultivated plants, the lily has been used for decoration, medicinal properties, and as a food in Asia Minor for more than four thousand years. Lilies are often given to brides or to women on their birthdays. In a culture that prizes male over female children, it is believed that this flower ensures the birth of a son.

Throughout history, the lily has been globally associated with divine goddesses. The flower is depicted as a symbol of fertility in Sumerian, Babylonian, Assyrian, Minoan, Egyptian, Greek, and Roman mythology. In Egyptian culture, the flower is an emblem of fertility and rebirth; drawings of lilies have been found on Egyptian tomb walls.

In the Roman Catholic tradition, the purity of the Virgin Mary has been compared to a white lily as far back as the seventh century. The lily appears near Mary in illuminated manuscripts from the Middle Ages and even more so in the Renaissance era. In Sandro Botticelli's painting *The Annunciation*, the archangel Gabriel holds the trumpet-shaped flowers as he kneels beside Mary, revealing that she will give birth to Christ. It has been said that Mary's tomb was covered with this flower, which is often called the Madonna lily. Roman Catholics, like the Egyptians and Chinese, associate the flower with notions of rebirth and resurrection, making it a popular flower during Easter celebrations.

MADDER

MAGNOLIA

M

Madder

CALUMNY

Madder has greenish blooms, but its red-yellow roots become a vivid red when pulverized into a powder. After munching on this flowering plant, sheep's teeth appear to be bloody. Fabric tinted with madder was found in King Tut's tomb, and the pigment was discovered in a paint shop in fossilized Pompeii. The Turkish people figured out a method to get the brightest results from the hue by mixing it with rancid castor oil, ox blood, and dung. In 1879, the invention of the synthetic alizarin crimson pigment rendered the Turkish recipe obsolete.

Magnolia

LOVE OF NATURE

The magnolia is an ancient flower believed to have existed before the appearance of bees—it was originally pollinated by beetles. An old superstition suggests that placing a magnolia under the bed ensures a partner's fidelity. For the same effect, some sewed magnolia leaves directly into the mattress. The perfume of this flower is so potent, legends warned that a single blossom in the bedroom could fatally overpower a person with its fragrance.

Magnolia glauca
Perseverance

Magnolia grandiflora
Dignity

Maltese Cross

SUN-BEAMING EYES

This vivid red flower is notable for its many names, including **flower of Bristol, Jerusalem cross, meadow campion,** and **scarlet Lychnis**. The name Maltese cross was chosen due to the bloom's resemblance to the heraldic cross associated with the Order of St. John and the island of Malta. Legend says that during the Crusades, it was the Knights of Malta who brought the plant from Jerusalem to England.

Manchineel Tree

FALSEHOOD

Also known as **Manzanilla de la Muerte**. A small drop of milky sap from this tree, dubbed "little apple of death" by the Spanish, is toxic. In 1521, Spaniard Juan Ponce de León led a colonizing expedition into the territory currently known as the Florida Everglades. In a battle with the Indigenous Calusa, Ponce de León was shot in the leg with an arrow tipped in manchineel sap. The Spaniards fled back to Cuba, where Ponce de León died shortly after.

Mandrake

RARITY

The roots of the mandrake plant have long been linked to magical lore due to their resemblance to the human body. Ancient Greeks considered the mandrake a phallic form that could be used to make love potions. Superstition states that when pulled from the ground, the human-like root shrieks so loudly that anyone in earshot will be killed from the sound. The safest extraction method was to tie a dog to the plant, and in time the sacrificial dog would run off, pulling the root from the soil.

MAPLE

MALTESE CROSS

MANCHINEEL TREE

MARIGOLD

MANDRAKE

Maple

RESERVE

There are more than a hundred types of maple, including Japanese, Norway, and paperback maples. Blooming in late winter, tiny blossoms appear in a variety of colors. The tapped sap from the sugar maple tree is boiled into sweet maple syrup. The Anishinaabe (Ojibwe)—native to southern Canada and the northern midwestern United States—call the syrup *zhiiwaagamizigan*.

Marigold

DESPAIR; GRIEF

Once known in Old English as Mary's gold, the French name for marigold is *souci*, which means "sorrow." Aware of calming properties in the flower, Aztecs used marigold, which they referred to as "the fog," to help calm anxiety. During the Victorian era, marigold cordial was prepared for those suffering from despair.

French Marigold
Jealousy

Kingcup Marigold
Desire for riches

Marjoram

BLUSHES

Native to the Mediterranean and western Asia, this herb was an ancient symbol of happiness for the Greeks and Romans. A favorite herb of Aphrodite, it was said that anointing oneself with fragrant marjoram would bring on dream visions of one's future spouse.

Marsh-Mallow

BENEFICENCE

The marsh-mallow root has been used in confections since the time of ancient Egyptians. During medieval trials in Europe, people were forced to prove their innocence by taking red-hot irons on their hands. Victims surreptitiously applied a thick paste of marsh-mallow sap, fleabane seeds, and egg whites to their palms to make the cruel test more bearable.

Marvel of Peru

TIMIDITY

In France, this colorful blossom is known as *belle de nuit* because the trumpet-shaped flare of these shy flowers opens to release their scent only in the evening. The unique musk emanating from this bushy shrub is not enjoyed by everyone. Flowers of various colors bloom on the same plant, and they can change color as they mature. Yellow blooms might transform into pink; white blooms, into a pale violet.

MARSH-MALLOW

MARJORAM

MEADOWSWEET

MARVEL OF PERU

MERCURY

MIGNONETTE

Meadowsweet

USELESSNESS

These fragrant flowers were a favorite of Queen Elizabeth I for strewing about onto floors. The fresh-cut herb would cover up any unpleasant odors. Originally named meadesweet or meadwort, it was an ingredient added to mead by Scottish brewers in the fourteenth century. Traces of the plant mixed with cremated remains were discovered in a four-thousand-year-old Welsh stone monument. The same burial ritual of combining meadowsweet with remains was uncovered in Bronze Age stone cists in the Orkney Islands.

Mercury

GOODNESS

The male and female mercury flowers grow on separate plants. Pollination occurs with the help of the wind. Mercury refers to the metallic element known as quicksilver and to the Roman god of communication. Linnaeus used graphic alchemical and planetary symbols to indicate the gender of plants. Venus was shorthand to mark plants as female; Mars, male; and Mercury, bisexual—or both male and female.

Mignonette

YOUR QUALITIES SURPASS YOUR CHARMS

The name for this humble but fragrant flower commonly used in Victorian perfumes and potpourris is taken from the French phrase "my young nun." Napoleon procured this shrub for his beloved Josephine during his campaign in Egypt. In nineteenth-century Europe, the mignonette was a popular choice to plant in window boxes to mask the less desirable city smells wafting in from the outside.

Milkvetch

YOUR PRESENCE SOFTENS MY PAIN

Also known as **Astragalus, Locoweed**. The name locoweed, meaning "crazy weed" in Spanish, refers to the reaction witnessed in livestock that consume this flower. Though it was once believed to have a positive effect on goat milk production, milkvetch is known to cause depression and neurological damage in some animals that eat this plant.

MILKVETCH

Milkwort

HERMITAGE

Hermits in the European Alps were known to plant milkwort around their solitary hideouts. Milkwort was once known as rogation flower, as it was used to decorate poles and garlands that were held during rogation week processions leading up to the Christian Feast of the Ascension.

Mimosa

SENSITIVENESS

MIMOSA

Also known as **Shame Plant, Sensitive Plant, Touch-Me-Not**. When the mimosa is touched, a protective reflex causes its leaves to fold up. Legend says that in 1886 Ethiopian empress Taytu Betul spotted a rare and beautiful flower and asked her husband, Emperor Menelik II, to build her a home on the flower's soil. In time, that very plot of land became the country's capital. The city's name, Addis Ababa, means "new flower" in Amharic. Some believe the capital city's name was inspired by this flower. Others say that although stunning, the mimosa flower, which was prevalent in the area, would have already been familiar to her.

MINT

MISTLETOE

MILKWORT

Mint

VIRTUE

A popular flavor for chewing gum, mints, toothpaste, and mouthwash, spearmint has long been used for its reputed antimicrobial and antiseptic properties. Recent studies suggest that memory and cognitive abilities might be improved if a student chews spearmint gum while they study. During medieval times, mint was used as a sanitizing aromatic. It was strewn into baths as well as around the home.

Peppermint
Warmth of sentiment

Mistletoe

I SURMOUNT ALL DIFFICULTIES

This parasitic shrub that grows along the tops of oaks and other trees is most well known for its Christmas tradition. Sprigs of mistletoe are hung in doorways during the holiday season, and if two people find themselves under it, they are to kiss. Pagan cultures viewed the shrub as a symbol of male fertility, with its white berries representing semen. Romans connected the plant with peace and love and hung it above doorways as a protective talisman.

Mock Orange

COUNTERFEIT

Named mock orange because of the blossoms' resemblance to flowers from orange and lemon trees, the scent of this shrub is also reminiscent of citrus and jasmine flowers. Sometimes referred to as **pipe tree**, the hollowed-out stems of this shrub have been used as smoking pipes by natives of western Canada as well as in Turkey.

Money Plant

HONESTY

The money plant blossoms with violet-colored flowers in the spring, followed by papery, translucent seedpods that look like silver coins. The Latin genus name *Lunaria* translates to "moon shaped." Bavarian doctor Johannes Hartlieb shared a recipe for witches' potion in *The Book of All Forbidden Arts, Heresy, and Sorcery* (1456), which included this plant. He recommended that for optimum potency, each plant should be picked on a particular day. This lunar flower was to be plucked on Mondays; the herb *Mercurialis* on Wednesdays; and turnsoles, or *solsequium*, on Sundays.

MOCK ORANGE

MONEY PLANT

MOONWORT

MONKSHOOD

MORNING GLORY

Monkshood

KNIGHT ERRANTRY

Also known as **Wolfsbane, Aconite**. A notorious poison, monkshood is known in herbal folklore as the "kiss of death." Arrow tips dipped in the plant's juice have been used in many cultures for hunting and warfare. Toward the end of the ancient Roman era, the plant was banned in parts of Europe due to an uptick in monkshood-related fatalities. The penalty for cultivating the helmet-shaped flowers was death.

Moonwort

FORGETFULNESS

After moonwort fades at the end of summer, it often lies dormant for many seasons, forgetting to regrow until it eventually decides to reappear. These spore-producing ferns can remain dormant underground for up to a year and sometimes longer.

Morning Glory

AFFECTION

A tea made from the seeds of the morning glory flower can produce an intoxicating effect comparable to a hallucinogenic LSD trip. Mayans used this floral tea to facilitate spiritual elucidation. Aztec priests used the seeds to induce psychedelic trances. Evidence of morning glory seeds, which were likely collected for healing rituals, has been found in vessels dating as far back as 250 CE.

Red Morning Glory
I attach myself to you

159 \ FLOWERS AND THEIR MEANINGS

Moschatel

WEAKNESS

Also known as **Five-Faced Bishop, Townhall Clock, Muskroot**. The moschatel, which favors a damp and shady habitat, is typically pollinated by snails. This five-sided flower appears to be looking out in every direction, resembling the outward faces of a town-square clock.

Moss

MATERNAL LOVE

In certain climates, moss is known for its ability to protect roots from the bitter cold. In preparation for a long winter indoors, Laplanders covered their underground homes in moss. Small birds have been known to line their nests with it, building a cozy home for their chicks.

Mossy Saxifrage

AFFECTION

Saxifraga means "stone breaker" in Latin. Thriving in rocky landscapes, it was first believed that this flowering plant received its name because it was known to grow out of the cracks in the stones. It turns out that it was used as a botanical tonic to get rid of kidney stones.

MOUNTAIN
LAUREL

MOSCHATEL

MOTHERWORT

160

MOSS

MOUNTAIN ASH

*MOSSY
SAXIFRAGE*

Motherwort

CONCEALED LOVE

In Japan, motherwort is associated with longevity. Japanese folklore tells of a village where everyone lived to be more than one hundred years old because their water source ran through a patch of motherwort. A festival celebrating the herbaceous plant takes place annually during the month of Kikousouki, where participants consume motherwort with rice and sake. "Drink motherwort to the despair of your heirs"—an old Japanese saying—became popular in Europe as the plant's popularity migrated west.

Mountain Ash

PRUDENCE

Also known as **Rowan, Witch Tree**. Found growing near ancient Druid sites and sacred rock formations, mountain ash was regarded with great veneration as a protector from evil spirits. The underside of the tree's bright red berries pucker to make the shape of the ancient five-pointed pentagram. Highland dairy maids used to drive cattle with a switch of mountain ash with the belief that it would protect the animals from danger.

Mountain Laurel

AMBITION

Also known as **Calico Bush, Spoonwood**. With showy clusters of white-and-pink bell flowers, the mountain laurel is not in the plant family of true laurels, *Laurus nobilis*, but the heather family, *Ericaceae*. The Cherokee use handfuls of bristly mountain laurel leaves to scratch the surface of the skin above an area suffering from rheumatoid arthritis. Then, leaf ooze is placed on top of the skin as an analgesic.

Moving Plant

AGITATION

Also known as **Dancing Plant**. Moving plant is one of the few plants capable of rapid movement; others include sensitive plant and the Venus flytrap. The hinged leaflets of this plant move rhythmically throughout the course of a day, with larger leaves slowly moving up and down and smaller leaves moving more quickly. Charles Darwin referred to this species as the **telegraph plant**, noticing a similarity to the semaphore telegraph, a machine with paddles that could be adjusted to broadcast specific messages from a distance.

Mugwort

HAPPINESS

Also known as **Artemisia**. Trota of Salerno was a trailblazing Italian female doctor in the late Middle Ages. It is said that her treatise on gynecology was widely circulated, garnering her fame in the twelfth and thirteenth centuries. The central herb in her pharmacy was mugwort, which she used as a contraceptive as well as an abortifacient. Modern scientific evidence shows some evidence to these claims. The camphor-scented herb is commonly used today in herbal yoni steaming.

MUGWORT

MULLEIN

MUSHROOM

MULBERRY BLOSSOM

MOVING PLANT

Mulberry Blossom

WISDOM

In the 1800s, white mulberry trees were brought to America from Asia with the intention to develop a silk industry. The project was abandoned, because the process—which involves raising silkworm caterpillars and unwinding their boiled cocoons in order to harvest silk—ended up being too laborious for Americans. Despite this, the trees flourished and now grow across the country.

Black Mulberry
I will not survive you

Mullein

HEALTH

Quaker women, who were forbidden to use makeup, used the yellow flowering mullein as an illicit beauty tool. Rubbing the soft hairy foliage from this plant on their cheeks triggered an allergic reaction that gave their pale complexions a rosy blush.

Mushroom

SUSPICION

Members of the kingdom of fungi, some mushrooms are delicious, some offer a psychedelic experience, and others are poisonous. Eurasian shamans from northern Siberia have been known to use the psychoactive fly agaric mushrooms. The red-capped toadstool mushrooms, which are covered in distinct white dots, are consumed to achieve a trance-like state. When the fungus passes through the renal system, its potent psychoactive elements are still present in the urine. Many resort to drinking the urine to reexperience the intoxicating effects.

163 \ FLOWERS AND THEIR MEANINGS

Musk Plant

WEAKNESS

Popular for its perfume, musk was widely cultivated during the Victorian era. Bizarrely, all known specimens began to lose their signature scent around 1913. There are several theories about this mysterious occurrence; perhaps it was the human ability to smell this plant that was lost or the scent had been caused by a parasite that no longer exists.

Mustard Seed

INDIFFERENCE

This plant is known in Sanskrit as "she-devil" or "witch" because at one time, Indians believed the mustard seed could be used to discover witches. During a nighttime ritual, mustard seed oil was dropped into a vessel of water while the name of each woman from the village was ceremoniously recited. If the shadow of a female form appeared in the water while a specific name was spoken, it was an indicator that the woman was a witch.

MYRTLE

MUSK PLANT

Myrobalan Plum

PRIVATION

Distinct from the juicy plum that may come to mind, this tree produces cherry-like fruit with an extremely unpleasant taste, also known as the *cherry plum*. This plant is in one of the early-twentieth-century homeopathic remedies produced by Bach Flower Remedies. This particular botanical essence was used to treat the overwhelming fear of losing control.

Myrtle

LOVE

The fragrant white puffs of the myrtle plant have been associated with love, duty, and affection since ancient times. Ovid described Venus as holding a stem of myrtle, which was believed to be an aphrodisiac, while emerging from the sea in a half shell. The ancient Roman festival Veneralia honored Venus Verticordia, an epithet of the goddess Venus, who was believed capable of inspiring chastity. Every April 1, her statue was taken from the temple to the men's baths, where female attendants undressed, washed, and then adorned it with garlands of myrtle.

MYROBALAN PLUM

MUSTARD SEED

N

Nasturtium

PATRIOTISM

In Greco-Roman times, warriors hung the armor of their fallen enemies from tree branches as a symbol of victory. The word *trophy*, as well as the Latin name for nasturtium, *Tropaeolum majus*, was derived from this type of monument, which was known as a *tropaion*. When naming the bright flower, Linnaeus was inspired by the leaves' resemblance to shields, and the petals to bloody helmets.

Scarlet Nasturtium
Warlike trophy

Nigella

PERPLEXITY

Also known as **Love in a Puzzle, Love-in-a-Mist, Jack in Prison**. The spiky blue or white flowers of nigella float among a mysterious cloud of misty, thread-like bract leaves. Native to the Middle East and the Mediterranean, the lacy foliage made its way to England and was a favorite in Elizabethan cottage gardens.

Night-Blooming Cereus

TRANSIENT BEAUTY

Also known as **Queen of the Night, Christ in the Manger**. The night-blooming cereus is a cactus that blooms only once a year for a single night; it is gone by sunrise. Sold in dry form, the flower is used in traditional Chinese medicine and to make a soup believed to detoxify the lungs.

NIGHT-BLOOMING CEREUS

NIGELLA

NASTURTIUM

OLEANDER

OATS, WILD

OLIVE BRANCH

OAK

O

Oak

HOSPITALITY

In ancient Rome, a crown of green oak was awarded for saving a Roman's life in battle. Customs stated that if a man wearing this crown entered a room, all must rise in his honor. Once a hero was bestowed with the green oak prize, he always had the right to wear it.

Evergreen Oak
Liberty

Oak Leaves
Bravery

White Oak
Independence

Oats, Wild

THE WITCHING SOUL OF MUSIC

The phrase "sowing your wild oats" dates to the sixteenth century and most likely referred to a weed that existed before the cultivated oats we think of today. The modern idiom captures young people's impulse to explore their wild side, having many sexual relationships before settling down, marrying, and/or having children.

Oleander

BEWARE!

A nineteenth-century legend tells of French soldiers waiting in an encampment who cut oleander branches to use as skewers to roast some meat. Twelve men died and five were seriously ill. Many versions of the same tale exist, and in 2005 researchers at the University of California–Irvine did an experiment to disprove this urban legend by using oleander skewers to cook hot dogs. Although the plant is undisputedly poisonous, the toxicological analysis revealed that with this method, the traces of deadly oleandrin extract were negligible and unlikely to do any harm.

Olive Branch

PEACE

See page 172.
The golden liquid extracted from olives was a key ingredient in ancient cosmetics. Some of the earliest eye shadows were made from pulverized minerals or charcoal mixed with olive oil. Hellenic athletes rubbed the oil all over their bodies before training in the nude. Aristotle recommended the use of olive oil, applied to the cervix, as a method of contraception in his *History of Animals*.

Orange Blossom

CHASTITY

Orange blossoms have long been associated with marriage. The Greek expression "go gathering orange blossoms" is a suggestion to go search for a wife. Princess Anne Marie Orsini of Nerola, the seventeenth-century Italian It Girl, was a big fan of the sweet-scented blossoms from the bitter orange tree. She insisted it perfume her gloves and baths; the essential oil became known as Neroli.

Orange
Generosity

Orchid

A BELLE

See page 174.
Orchid bulbs, which look like testicles, are associated with sex and virility. In the Ottoman Empire, it was served as an aphrodisiac concoction in the eighth century. The tubers were ground into a powder, known as salep, which was the key ingredient in the beverage *sahlab*. In the seventeenth century, it became popular in Britain and Germany as "saloop" before losing popularity in the nineteenth century when it was rumored to be a cure for sexually transmitted diseases. Served hot with milk and lots of cinnamon, *sahlab* is still a popular winter treat in Turkey.

Bee Orchid
Industry

Butterfly Orchid
Gaiety

Cattleya Orchid
Mature charms

Comet Orchid
Royalty

ORANGE BLOSSOM

OSMUNDA

Fly Orchid
Error

Frog Orchid
Disgust

Lady's Slipper Orchid
Capricious beauty

Spider Orchid
Adroitness

Osmunda

DREAMS

A stately flowering fern, *Osmunda* is believed to hold magical powers. According to Slavic legend, any person who collects a frond will gain the ability to fend off demons. The catch? The only way to obtain a frond is to draw a circle around the fern, step inside, and then endure demonic taunts.

FLY ORCHID

ORCHID

Olive

PEACE

See page 169

To "extend an olive branch" is a figure of speech indicating a willingness and desire to set aside differences and end a conflict. The olive has long been a sacred tree used for benedictions, rituals of purification, and as a representation of eternal hope.

In ancient Greece, garlands woven from various plants were presented to champions in both battle and sport. Competitors at the Pythian Games were awarded with laurel garlands; parsley was presented at the Nemean Games; and pine was given at the Elean Games. Victors at the Olympian Games were presented with wild olive garlands. Olive oil burned in the lamp of the original Olympic torch of eternal flame.

The Al Badawi olive tree, perhaps the oldest olive tree alive, grows on contested land, near Bethlehem in occupied Palestine. It is named after an Egyptian Sufi who spent much of his time relaxing under the tree's very branches. The tree was carbon-dated in 2010 and appears to be between 3,000 and 5,500 years old. No one knows for certain, but it likely predates the existence of Islam, Christianity, and Judaism.

The Hebrew Bible introduces olive leaves as a hopeful symbol of peace in the book of Genesis. When a dove brings Noah a sprig of olive, the flood is over. During the Jewish festival of Hanukkah, celebrants eat latkes, donuts, and other foods fried in olive oil. The oil is used to honor the legend of a miracle that took place in Jerusalem during the second century BCE. Living under the oppressive rule of King Antiochus IV Epiphanes, Jews were forbidden to practice their religion and were forced to worship the Greek gods. During a bloody massacre, the Second Temple on the Mount was desecrated and looted. After a successful rebellion, the Jews set out to reconsecrate their sacred temple. Despite the small amount of the oil left in the temple's seven-branched menorah, the emblematic eternal flame inexplicably kept burning for eight days.

Orchid

A BELLE

See page 170

Named for the flower's tubular roots, the word *orchid* is derived from the Greek *orkihis*, meaning "testicle." The ancient Greeks believed that the shapely sap-filled roots were an aphrodisiac that would simultaneously strengthen the body and "provoketh Venus." It was also believed that a pregnant woman could use the flower to influence the gender of her baby. Eating a large root was supposed to ensure that the baby would be male; a smaller root, female.

Many orchid species visually mirror the insect that pollinates them. The bee orchid, for example, is a sexually deceptive perennial. It lures pollinators by releasing a chemical closely mimicking the insect's sex pheromones. It also offers a fuzzy labellum petal, which resembles a female bee. Once the male bee "mates" with the orchid, he will be coated with lots of pollen to carry elsewhere.

The nectar of the comet orchid of Madagascar is located at the bottom of narrow spurs, which go as deep as twelve inches. Charles Darwin suspected the pollinator of this flower must have a proboscis (a tubular sucking organ) of equal length or longer. In 1862, people thought this hypothesis was ridiculous. More than forty years later, the nearby hawk moth of Madagascar was identified as the comet orchid's natural pollinator. It boasts a proboscis that ranges from eight to fourteen inches in length when unraveled from the moth's mouth.

175

\ FLOWERS AND THEIR MEANINGS

P

Palm

VICTORY

In the Mediterranean and Near East regions, this foliage has long symbolized victory and triumph. Palm fronds were awarded to victorious athletes in Greece. In ancient times, palm branches were carried in warlike processions to announce victory over an enemy.

Pansy

THOUGHTS

See page 178.
Folklore surrounding pansies as a method of fortune-telling allegedly traces back to the time of King Arthur. Pluck an upper petal and the number of visible veins was believed to correspond with your fate. Four veins signified hope, seven confirmed forever love, eight veins meant fickle love. Count to eleven and be warned: The beholder's love would suffer an early death.

Purple Pansy
You occupy my thoughts

Wild Pansy (Heartsease)
Love in idleness

Yellow-and-Purple Mixed Pansy
Forget me not

PALM

PANSY

Pansy

THOUGHTS

see page 176

The pansy is connected to notions of thought and memory for a simple reason of phonetics. *Pansy* sounds like the French word *penser*, "to think." With velvety heart-shaped petals, the thoughts conjured by these blooms are of a tender and affectionate nature.

The flower's name has also been used throughout history as a derogatory term to shame effeminate and homosexual men. Evoking the delicate nature of the bloom, the slur suggests a dainty lack of masculinity. Of the countless species that share this quality, why the pansy?

The leaves of this flower were once used by the Celts to brew a love potion tea. Perhaps Shakespeare had this ancient folk concoction in mind when he wrote *A Midsummer Night's Dream*. The pansy's powers, in Shakespeare's writing, were bestowed by Cupid's bow, whose arrow pierced a white flower, turning it "purple with love's wound." Oberon, the Fairy King, dripped pansy juice onto the eyes of sleeping Queen Titania, with whom he had been quarreling. Such a trick was thought to "make man or woman madly dote on the next live creature that it sees. . . . Be it on lion, bear, or wolf, or bull, on meddling monkey, or on busy ape." Titania falls in love with an Athenian weaver whose head has been replaced with that of a donkey. Could it be that the modern homophobic label borrows the floral sentiment described in the play—the idea that "pansies" fall in love so indiscriminately that they might

even set their sights on a creature as "inappropriate" as someone of the same gender?

For a fleeting moment, pansy purple was widely advertised as the new "it" color. In 1924, *Vogue* magazine recommended the hue for the smartest autumnal hats, and purple apparel was produced in large quantities, rendering the hue passé almost immediately. The trend died just as massive orders of golf suits and neckwear hit the menswear market. The resulting attitude was that only a foppish dandy or flamboyant fashion victim would dare sport a pansy tie.

These cultural associations entwined the pansy with femme queerness. The flower was weaponized as a slur. During the 1920s and '30s, however, the term's negativity was powerfully upended by the celebratory Pansy Craze. During Prohibition, gay-owned bars and cabarets popped up in New York City. The Pansy Club was a speakeasy and a venue for vibrant entertainment, including glamorous drag performances such as "Pansies on Parade." Reclaiming the slur, the illicit bars were popular with a variety of patrons, including curious cultural tourists and those seeking a forbidden sip. The gayness of it all was considered tolerable by conservative patrons who interpreted the performance style to be a form of vaudeville, which was an art form already familiar to them. After a series of police raids, gang shootings, and issues with mob affiliated landlords, this blossoming performance culture and its public celebrations of queerness retreated underground.

Parsley

FESTIVITY

Ancient Greeks and Romans used parsley to crown victors and to adorn graves. The herb is often used as one of the six symbolic foods on the seder plate used for Passover. During the ceremonial meal, the greens—referred to as karpas—represent hope and renewal. Parsley is ritualistically dipped in salt water—representing tears—before being eaten to symbolize the pain of the Hebrew slaves in Egypt. When consumed, the pain and new birth are symbolically tasted at once.

Pasque Flower

YOU HAVE NO CLAIM

Derived from *pasakh*, the Hebrew word for Passover, the pasque flower is often connected to Easter, Passover, rebirth, and the spring season. Legend says that this flower only blooms in soil soaked with the blood of Roman or Dane soldiers.

PASSION FLOWER

PARSLEY

PASQUE FLOWER

FLOWERS AND THEIR MEANINGS \

PEACH BLOSSOM

PEAR BLOSSOM

Passion Flower

RELIGIOUS SUPERSTITION

When Jesuit fathers and conquistadores arrived in South America in the sixteenth century, a native flowering vine reminded them of Jesus's crucifixion. The five stamens represented the five wounds of Jesus; the five petals and five sepals together represented the ten faithful apostles; the corona, the crown of thorns; the three pistils, the nails used to hang him on the cross. Lastly, the ovary was said to represent the goblet of the Lord. The Indigenous people had long enjoyed eating the delicious yellow fruit of the vine. The Jesuits interpreted this as a sign that they were hungry for Christianity.

Peach Blossom

I AM YOUR CAPTIVE

Native to northwestern China, this deciduous tree bears juicy peaches and nectarines. More than half the world's supply of this fruit comes from China. Early Chinese rulers used peach tree rods to protect themselves from evil forces. It was believed that ghosts were afraid of this particular wood. In preparation for the New Year, magistrates placed peach branches over their doors for protection, and citizens had magic wands made from peach tree wood.

Pear Blossom

COMFORT

In some regions of Germany and Switzerland, it was tradition to plant a tree at a wedding and then again for the birth of each child. In honor of a baby boy, an apple tree was planted, and for a baby girl it was a pear tree.

Pennycress

INFLEXIBILITY

Considered a common weed across Eurasia and much of America, pennycress sports tiny white, lavender, or pink flowers as well as flat green pods that hold dark oval seeds. The round pods are coin size and resemble the old English penny. Pennycress has proven to decontaminate soil from heavy metals, such as zinc and cadmium.

Pennyroyal

FLEE AWAY!

Pennyroyal has a long history of being used as a traditional folk remedy to stimulate menstruation as well as an abortifacient. The herbal tea is toxic and highly dangerous. Kurt Cobain's unused liner notes for the song "Pennyroyal Tea" on Nirvana's 1993 album *In Utero* state, "herbal abortive . . . it doesn't work, you hippie." The song, which explores his chronic depression, was scheduled to be released as a single in April 1994, the same month that Cobain committed suicide. With a B-side titled "I Hate Myself and Want to Die," the release was canceled.

PEONY

PENNYROYAL

FLOWERS AND THEIR MEANINGS \

PENNYCRESS

PERIWINKLE

Peony

BASHFUL; SHAME

The association between peonies and bashfulness originated from folklore that told of mischievous nymphs hiding within the peony's numerous petals. In China, the flower is a symbol of wealth and rank. The only woman to have ruled in China was Empress Wu Zetian, who reigned at the turn of the eighth century. Disappointed that no flowers were on display during her winter stroll in the imperial garden, she issued a decree for them to bloom. The following day, according to legend, all flowers complied—except for the peonies. Infuriated, she had the defiant peonies burned. They were so resilient, however, that they sprouted beautiful red flowers. Exasperated, she banished the flowers to the city of Luoyang.

Periwinkle

TENDER RECOLLECTIONS

An evergreen ground cover, periwinkle is a flowering, trailing vine, meaning it does not twine or climb. In Europe, the bloom received the morbid moniker "flower of death" because long ago crowns of periwinkle were placed on dead children. Catholics considered the periwinkle a "virgin" flower because of its blue hue—which ostensibly linked the blossoms to the Virgin Mary. In the nineteenth century, the wildflower was frequently scattered over the graves of enslaved African Americans.

Blue Periwinkle
Early friendship

White Periwinkle
Pleasures of memory

Persimmon Blossom

BURY ME AMID NATURE'S BEAUTIES

Old plantation songs from the eighteenth-century American South describe the enjoyment of persimmon beer. Without access to fresh and clean water, enslaved workers drank the fermented beverage to quench their thirst. A formerly enslaved man named West Turner recorded a recipe for the sour drink: Sweet potato peels and hunks of cornbread were added to fermenting persimmons in a barrel of water.

PINE

Phlox

UNANIMITY

The name *phlox* is derived from the Greek word for "flame" or "light." Growing in elongated clusters, cultivars of this bloom include intense colors, including Starfire (crimson), Prince of Orange, and Velvet Flame (hot purple). Superstition says that singles looking for love should plant this delicate flower in their garden or bring them into their home.

Pieris Japonica

FAIRIES' FIRE

Traditionally, this Japanese native was planted in tea gardens connected to temples and shrines. The wood could be used as charcoal in the hearth where an iron kettle was set to boil. Rarely seen as a single shrub, the *Pieris japonica* was generally planted in groupings under trees. It is recognized for its drooping clusters of white flowers and unique leaves, which sometimes emerge as a flaming bronze red but transition to a dark, glossy green.

PINEAPPLE

PIERIS JAPONICA

PHLOX

PERSIMMON BLOSSOM

Pine

PITY

The scales of the pinecone spiral in a perfect Fibonacci sequence. The human pineal gland, which is linked to sleep patterns and the perception of light, is located at the center of the brain and is named for the pinecone. Philosophers around the globe revered the pineal gland as sacred or mystical, some even referring to it as a biological "third eye."

Pineapple

YOU ARE PERFECT

In 1496, Christopher Columbus returned from his trip to the Americas with a pineapple, provoking a European fascination with the South American fruit. The Europeans did not have any luck propagating them, and so the pineapple became an expensive, rare delicacy. To impress their guests, European socialites would rent a pineapple to display at a gathering before returning it, whole and untasted. The coveted fruit was similarly difficult to acquire in the American colonies until railroads were installed. By 1860, they were being grown in Florida, and at the turn of the century, canned fruit was being shipped for mass consumption.

Pink

BOLDNESS

A member of the *Dianthus* family, which includes the carnation and sweet William, this flower is likely how the color got its name. The saw-toothed scissors that snip a perfectly zigzag edge—pinking shears—are probably named after the jagged edges of pink petals. Before these specialty scissors were patented by Louis Austin in 1893, pinking was done with punches or irons hammered with a mallet.

China Pink
Aversion

Garden Pink
Childishness

Mountain Pink
Aspiring

Red Pink
Pure and ardent love

Striped Pink
Refusal

White Pink
Talent

Yellow Pink
Disdain

PLUM BLOSSOM

PLANE

PINK

PINWHEEL FLOWER

Pinwheel Flower

PAINTING

Also known as **Crape Jasmine, Indian Carnation**. Despite its common names, these crisp white flowers are neither carnation nor jasmine. Native to South Asia, it is known as *Chandni* flower in Hindi. The Bower Manuscript is a fragmented collection of Sanskrit medical and divination commentary from the sixth century, and the text lists this flower as an ingredient in amrit, the legendary drink of the devas, said to grant immortality.

Plane

GENIUS

In ancient Greece, the plane tree was an emblem of genius because Athenian philosophers participated in discourse under the shade of these tall trees. In 480 BCE, King Xerxes of Persia saw a plane tree for the first time. He was so enthralled by it, he halted his army while he hung all his jewels on its branches. He also removed the adornments from his concubines and the lords in his entourage to add to the glittering tree, which he declared his goddess.

Plum Blossom

KEEP YOUR PROMISES

Plum blossoms bloom during the transition of winter into spring, bringing the promise of fruitfulness. According to Japanese folklore, the plum holds powers to protect from evil. It is believed that evil will enter a garden from the northeast, so a plum tree is traditionally planted in that corner to protect the negative spirits from entering.

Wild Plum
Independence

Poinsettia

BRILLIANCY

The poinsettia was originally cultivated for medicinal use by the Aztecs. The flower's contemporary association with Christmas traces back to a sixteenth-century Mexican legend. A young girl named Pepita, who could not afford a celebratory gift to honor Jesus's birthday, was instructed by an angel to gather weeds from the side of the road and present them at the church altar. Crimson flowers bloomed from the weeds—the star-shaped leaves symbolizing the star of Bethlehem.

Pomegranate Blossom

MATURE ELEGANCE

The oldest evidence of pomegranate cultivation is from 2200 BCE in what is now Iraq. The pomegranate has been noted in ancient Jewish, Islamic, and Christian religious manuscripts, as well as Chinese and Hindu medicinal texts. In Greek mythology, Persephone chooses to eat six of the pomegranate seeds offered to her by Hades, cementing her obligation to return to the underworld for six months of every year. An ancient Armenian custom is to give a bride a pomegranate to throw against a wall. If many seeds scatter, it is a sign of many children in her future.

Pomegranate
Foolishness

POINSETTIA

POPLAR

*POMEGRANATE
BLOSSOM*

POPPY

Poplar

COURAGE; TIME

The demigod Hercules wrapped a branch of poplar around his head as a signal of his victory after vanquishing the fire-breathing giant Cacus. Garlands fashioned from poplar foliage were worn by Hercules's worshippers whenever they performed ceremonial sacrifices in his honor.

Black Poplar
Courage

White Poplar
Time

Poppy

CONSOLATION

See page 192.
After World War I, wild red poppies sprang up over the makeshift graves of fallen soldiers killed in battle. The poppy became the symbol of Remembrance Day, observed by the Commonwealth of Nations, in honor of the sacrifice these soldiers made. The French felt similarly about poppies and had since the Napoleonic Wars. Battle disturbs the soil in a way that increases its lime content; while these conditions are less than favorable for most flowers, the poppy happily flourished.

California Poppy
Do not refuse me

Scarlet Poppy
Fantastic extravagance

Variegated Poppy
Flirtation

White Poppy
Sleep. My bane, my antidote

189

Potato Blossom

BENEVOLENCE

Cultivated by the Inca for thousands of years, there are more than four thousand varieties of potatoes grown in Peru alone. Spanish conquistadores brought the nightshade to Europe in the sixteenth century. Two centuries later, Frenchman and potato promoter Antoine-Augustin Parmentier arranged many publicity stunts to convince the hesitant European population to give the nutritious tubers a chance. Marie Antoinette is said to have worn potato blossoms in her hair as part of this campaign, and Benjamin Franklin was one of the celebrity guests at a glamorous potato-themed dinner.

Primrose

EARLY YOUTH

Also known as **Polyanthus**. In much of his work, Shakespeare presented the primrose as a flower for the funerals of young people and for young women in particular. Up until the nineteenth century, chlorosis, also known as "maid's malady," was a deadly disease that turned the skin a hue of yellowish green. An old legend told that unmarried young women who succumbed to this fate would transform into a primrose flower.

Lilac Primrose
Confidence

Red Primrose
Unpatronized merit

PRIVET

PRIMROSE

*PUMPKIN
BLOSSOM*

*POTATO
BLOSSOM*

Privet

PROHIBITION

In 1941, the British government mandated that all iron gates older than one hundred years be removed and donated to produce weaponry for World War II. All across the country, privet bushes became a popular natural alternative to fences and borders. Metal stubs of sawed-off posts can still be found, peeking out from under privet foliage across the United Kingdom today.

Pumpkin Blossom

GROSSNESS

A nutritional mainstay of Native populations in North and South America, pumpkin seeds have been found in caves in Oaxaca, Mexico, dating back ten thousand years. At the 1900 World's Fair, held in Paris, a 400-pound pumpkin set a world record. In 2014, it was far surpassed by a Swiss pumpkin weighing in at 2,323 pounds— more than a ton. *Cucurbita maxima*, the variety we know as the giant pumpkin, is likely the largest of all fruit and vegetables.

Poppy

CONSOLATION

See page 189

Opium, morphine, and heroin are all derived from the narcotic sap of the opium poppy. Fossil recordings of seeds from this flower have been found in the Mediterranean, dating back to the early Neolithic Age. The seeds have even been found in the teeth of a man from that time. The flower's sap has been used as a recreational, medicinal, and ceremonial drug for a very long time.

Ancient Egyptian hieroglyphic writings suggest the opium poppy was used as a method of pain relief during childbirth. It is also listed in the Ebers Papyrus, a medicinal text from 1550 BCE, as a way to soothe a crying infant. Imagery of this flower growing in fields has captivated the human imagination since ancient times. In ancient Egypt, the poppy was associated with Osiris, the god of the dead. Chopping down grains while harvesting the fields was symbolically seen as the death of Osiris. Red corn poppies would soon pop up in the freshly shorn pastures, looking like splotches of blood.

At the beginning of the nineteenth century, the East India Trading Company waged a trade war with China. The British were frustrated that China was not buying goods from them, despite the large orders they were placing, so they started to smuggle loads of addictive opium into China. This resulted in millions of Chinese people becoming hooked on the drug. China responded to this situation by trying to stop trade altogether. The conflict is known as the Opium War.

The sale of heroin was made illegal in America in 1923, and possession of the drug was criminalized the following year. Technically, it is legal to possess the seeds. The opium poppy is the only Schedule II narcotic that you can purchase at a store and grow in your backyard. The U.S. Drug Enforcement Administration has been asking garden centers to stop selling seeds since 1995, but the requests are mostly ignored. The papery petals make for such a pretty addition to any landscape. Consumed in small quantities, the seeds are totally harmless—however, a few slices of poppy seed cake could accidentally result in a positive drug test.

RAGWEED

Q

Queen Anne's Lace

DO NOT REFUSE ME

Also known as **Wild Carrot**. At the center of this flower's delicate white filigree is one red dot. This is thought to represent a drop of blood from Queen Anne of Britain, as if she pricked her finger with a needle while making lace.

*QUEEN
ANNE'S LACE*

R

RANUNCULUS

RAGGED-ROBIN

Ragged-Robin

WIT

The petals of these bright pink blooms form a ragged, wispy star shape. Their preferred habitats are damp meadows or forests as well as bog gardens. Some say that if ragged-robin flowers are picked and brought inside, bad luck, undesirable weather, and thunder are soon to follow.

Ragweed

LOVE RETURNED

Also known as **Ambrosia**. A single ragweed plant can produce as many as a billion grains of pollen in a single season. The particles of this common allergen remain airborne for days and travel miles, causing suffering for many people with allergies. Higher levels of carbon dioxide in the atmosphere cause higher amounts of pollen to be released; climate change will continue to intensify the issue.

Ranunculus

I AM DAZZLED BY YOUR CHARMS

The name *Ranunculus* is derived from the Latin for "little frog." The flower, like the amphibian, can often be found by the water. Roman philosopher Apuleius of the first century CE believed that hanging the roots of the flower wrapped in linen around one's neck was a dependable cure for lunacy.

Garden Ranunculus
You are rich in attractions

Wild Ranunculus
Ingratitude

Raspberry Blossom

REMORSE

Native to Asia, these delicious berries came to North America along with prehistoric migrants. The leaves were used by many Indigenous cultures to make a medicinal tea. The caffeine-free infusion has a pleasing flavor similar to black tea. In 1773, American colonial merchants staged the Boston Tea Party protest, dumping the British East India Trading Company's tea into the ocean. In search of a new source of tea, New England settlers favored the accessible raspberry and sage teas made from local plants.

Reeds

MUSIC

In Greek mythology, a nymph named Syrinx was being chased by the satyr Pan. When she was stopped by the river Ladon, she pleaded for help from her watery sisters. Just as Pan grasped her, she transformed into tall, hollow marsh reeds. Noticing the nice sound of the wind passing through the reeds, Pan cut various lengths of the stems to create the pan flute. The reeds used for modern woodwind instruments, such as the clarinet or bassoon, are traditionally sourced from the giant reed plant.

Feathery Reeds
Indiscretion

Flowering Reeds
Confidence in heaven

RHODODENDRON

RESTHARROW

REEDS

Restharrow

OBSTACLE

The final step of manufacturing a medieval Russian sword made from bulat steel was to dip the weapon into a vat containing spiny restharrow extract. It was believed that the liquefied plant helped strengthen the metal. The original method is lost, and contemporary scientists have not been able to find any metallurgical properties in restharrow.

Rhododendron

DANGER

Some rhododendron species are poisonous—to varying degrees—to both animals and humans. Eating the poisonous rosebay rhododendron leaves could lead to convulsions and even a coma. A fourth-century BCE Greek text tells of ten thousand soldiers being poisoned with rhododendron honey. Ralph Waldo Emerson's 1834 poem "The Rhodora, on Being Asked, Whence Is the Flower," presents the rhododendron as a humble flower that, unlike its rival, the rose, does not seek out fame despite its beauty. The poem explores a spiritual connection to God, forged through nature.

RASPBERRY BLOSSOM

Rhubarb

ADVICE

Rhubarb has been used medicinally in Asia for more than five thousand years. The name comes from the Latin *rhababarum*, "root of the barbarians," which indicates the Roman view of those who ate it. Highly valued as a curative in seventeenth-century England, rhubarb was twice as expensive as opium. Benjamin Franklin is credited with bringing the rhubarb to America at the end of the eighteenth century, but it wasn't until a hundred or so years later that England and America began using it in their cuisine.

Rockrose

POPULAR FAVOR

Also known as **Cistus**. The clear fragrant resin of this flowering plant was greatly valued by the ancients. A sticky brown substance called labdanum coats the plant's leaves and is used medicinally and for cosmetics. Lured by the aromatic resin, goats bite into the branches, causing the substance to flow freely from the punctures. The resin is combed off the beards of the grazing goats and used to make perfume.

Gum *Cistus*
I shall die tomorrow

ROCKROSE

RHUBARB

Rose

LOVE

See page 204.
The rose has long held a uniquely elevated status in the hearts and minds of flower lovers across the globe. The ancient world loved to luxuriate in roses. In ancient Egypt, Cleopatra once purchased enough roses to fill a hall with an eighteen-inch-deep carpet of velvety petals to seduce Marc Antony. In the Hindu tradition, the goddess Laxmi is said to have been created from precisely 108 large roses and 1,008 small petals. Both Greek and Persian mythology link the rose's red color to blood.

Austrian Rose
Thou art all that is lovely

Bicolor Rose
Scandal; Study

Bridal Rose
Happy love

Burgundy Rose
Unconscious beauty

Cabbage Rose
Ambassador of love

China Rose
Beauty always new

Cinnamon Rose
Precocity

Damask Rose
Brilliant complexion

Deep Pink Rose
Encouragement

Deep Red Rose
Bashful shame

Dog Rose
Pleasure and pain

DOG ROSE

MOSS ROSEBUD

YELLOW ROSE

ROSE

DAMASK ROSE

CHINA ROSE

Full-Blown Rose Over Two Buds
Secrecy

Maiden Blush Rose
If you love me, you will find it out

Moss Rose
Voluptuousness

Moss Rosebud
Confession of love

Multiflora Rose
Grace

Musk Rose
Capricious beauty

Pompom Rose
Genteel prettiness

Red and White Rose
Fires of the heart

Red and White Roses (together)
Unity

Red Rose
Love

Red Rosebud
Pure and lovely

Rosa Mundi
Variety

Rose Leaf
I will never beg

Rosebud
Young girl; Heart which ignores love

Striped Rose
Summer

Sweet Briar Rose
Poetry; I wound to heal

Thornless Rose
Sincere friend

White Rose
Silence

White Rose (dried)
Death preferable to loss of innocence

White Rose (withered)
Transient impressions

White Rosebud
Girlhood

Wild Rose
Simplicity

Withered Rose
Fleeting beauty

Yellow Rose
Jealousy; infidelity

Yellow Sweet Briar Rose
Decrease of love

Rose of Sharon

CONSUMED BY LOVE

For centuries, this cousin to the hibiscus has held special meaning in Korea. Known as the *mugunghwa*, it signifies "eternal blossom that never fades." During the Japanese occupation of the early twentieth century, the bloom became a symbol of Korean resistance. In 1933, teacher Nam Gung-eok was arrested and imprisoned for sending tens of thousands of rose of Sharon flowers across the land. After regaining independence, the rose of Sharon became the national flower of South Korea.

Rosemary

REMEMBRANCE

Rosemary has been associated with death since ancient times, when it was used in the Egyptian embalming process. Sprigs have been discovered in tombs dating back to 3000 BCE. It was once the custom in France to place rosemary in the hand of the deceased before sealing the coffin. The herb has also been said to revive mental abilities, especially those related to memory. Students in ancient Greece would braid the herb in their hair or tuck a sprig behind their ear as a stimulant to assist them during exams.

ROSE OF SHARON

RUSHES

RUE

ROSEMARY

Rue

DISDAIN

It is the bitter taste of this plant that conjures the negative sentiment "disdain." In several cultures, rue is connected to a young woman's virginity and the idea that she will regret losing it. The Sephardic folk song "Una matica de ruda" (A sprig of rue) describes a flowering sprig given to a girl from a doting fellow. The girl's mother implores her not to fall into ruin with a young lover, suggesting that a bad husband would be preferable. The daughter insists a bad husband is a horrible curse, but "a young lover, Mother, is an apple or a lemon."

Rushes

DOCILITY

A family of flowering plants, hundreds of species of rush grow across the globe. In medieval Europe, sweet rushes were strewn all over dirt floors in lieu of carpets. Perhaps it was for the aroma, or perhaps the plant's density was helpful in keeping feet dry in damp weather. Henry VIII's chaplain, Cardinal Thomas Wolsey, had his floor rushes replaced every day. Soft rush is used to weave tatami mats in Japan. Indigenous Australians used a particular rush species for fishing lines and fiber, making woven rugs and sturdy woven baskets from the grass-like plant.

Rose

LOVE

See page 200

In ancient Greek mythology, Eros, the Greek god of love, gave a rose to Harpocrates, the god of silence, to guarantee discretion around Aphrodite's reckless activities. Harpocrates is often depicted in the nude, covering his lips with a forefinger—"Shhh!" The rose remained a symbol of secrecy up through the Middle Ages. A rose motif was often carved or painted on the ceiling directly above a table as a signal that anything said at the table was to be held in strict confidence and not to be repeated. The old Latin phrase *sub rosa* literally translates to "under the rose" and means secrecy. A rose would also appear above Roman Catholic confessionals.

Father Christian Rosencreuz (rose cross) was the semimythical founder of the Rosicrucian Order. The lore tells that he traveled widely, studying the esoteric wisdom of Turkish, Arab, and Persian sages. He died in complete secret, and 120 years later his pristine body was discovered by a member of the brotherhood, in a heptagonal vault. This was all shared in *Fama fraternitatis*, the manifesto of this order, which was anonymously written in Germany in 1614. The emblem of the Rosicrucians is the Rosy Cross. One interpretation is that the rose represents silence, and the cross represents salvation.

The word *rosary* is derived from the Latin *rosarium*, meaning "garland of roses." One method of creating these Catholic prayer beads is with roses themselves: The petals are chopped, soaked, and stewed, and the resulting floral clay is formed into beads. Some people create rosaries from flowers saved from a funeral or other solemn event as a sentimental keepsake.

The epitome of Byzantine architecture, the Hagia Sophia, was once the world's largest cathedral. Legend says that when Sultan Mehmed II conquered Istanbul in 1453, he had the massive church washed and purified in rose water before converting it into a mosque.

SAGE

SAINFOIN

S

Sage

DOMESTIC VIRTUE

Sage has long been venerated by many cultures across the globe. White sage is a specific species that is considered sacred for many indigenous cultures of the Americas. Used for smudging, leaves are bundled together and burned to produce fragrant ceremonial smoke that is spiritually cleansing. Smudging sage has become so popular outside of Native communities that the plant is now being overharvested. A respectful alternative would be to burn lavender or pine.

Sainfoin

AGITATION

The Greek name for this genus, *Onobrychis*, means something like "devoured by donkey." Sainfoin helps fatten up the large grazing mammals that eat it, as well as reduce the animals' methane emissions. Also known as **holy hay**, a French legend describes the pink flowers forming themselves into a halo around the head of baby Jesus.

Salvia

WISDOM

Closely related to sage, *Salvia* features aromatic clusters of spiky blossoms, but it is the large velvety green leaves that contain hallucinogenic compounds. These flowering plants are native to isolated cloud forests in Oaxaca, Mexico. The Mazatec shamans of the region have a tradition of carefully facilitating healing ceremonies where the leaves are eaten. Elsewhere, *Salvia* is smoked. Common effects include visual distortion, synesthesia, and disassociation from reality.

Red *Salvia*
Energy

Scabiosa

UNFORTUNATE ATTACHMENT

Also known as **Pincushion Flower**. Once used to treat the itchy condition of scabies, the name *Scabiosa* is derived from the Latin *scabere*, meaning "to scratch." An ointment made from the root was used in the seventeenth century to treat wounds, snakebites, and the plague. The shape of this attractive bloom resembles a pincushion with many pins sticking out of it.

Mourning Bride (Sweet *Scabiosa*)
Widowhood; I have lost all

SCARLET PIMPERNEL

SCABIOSA

SCURVY-GRASS

RED SALVIA

Scarlet Pimpernel

ASSIGNATION

Also known as **Peasant's Barometer, Shepherd's Weather Glass**. Despite its name, the scarlet pimpernel doesn't appear only in red. There are a wide variety of colors, including persimmon orange, azure blue, lilac, and white varieties. The flower is a trusted forecast for precipitation. Its petals remain open when the weather is sunny and dry; if they are shut, wet weather is on its way.

Scurvy-Grass

UTILITY

Known for its strong horseradish taste, this grass was eaten to prevent scurvy. It doesn't have a particularly high content of vitamin C, but it is easy to identify and grows throughout all four seasons along coastlines, making it a useful plant for sailors spending long intervals out at sea. In the first century CE, Pliny the Elder described Roman soldiers suffering from an affliction. The symptoms were similar to scurvy, and many believe that his prescribed cure, *Herba britannica*, was the plant we now know as scurvy-grass.

Sedum

TRANQUILITY

Also known as **Stonecrop**. *Sedum* is planted as an ornamental garden plant and used on green roof gardens due to its bright geometric blooms and general hardiness. It has also been used for generations for nutritional and medicinal purposes by Indigenous people of the Pacific Northwest. An infusion made from *Sedum* flowers and leaves was used by the Sylix (Okanagan) people to clean out the womb after childbirth. The Nlaka'pamux (Thompson) tribe have used a decoction of the plant as a sedative, and it is used as a salad green by the Haida and Nisga'a peoples.

Service Tree

PRUDENCE

Also known as **Sorb Tree**. In Plato's *Symposium,* the apple-shaped fruit of the service tree is used to describe when Zeus split the original spherical humans in two. In ancient Greece, the fruit was typically cut in half and pickled. If the fruit is to be consumed raw, it is typically put aside to overripen, soften, and sweeten. At this near-rotten stage, this fruit is its most delicious.

Shooting Star

YOU ARE MY DIVINITY

Also known as **Dodecatheon.** The gracefully nodding shooting star flower appears to be in midflight, resembling a badminton birdie, feathered dart, or shooting star. When taken orally from a dropper, the essence of this flower is purported to help those who feel deep alienation from their human family or who have suffered intense birthing trauma.

SNAKEROOT

SHOOTING STAR

SERVICE TREE

SNAPDRAGON

SEDUM

Snakeroot

HORROR

In the nineteenth century, a mysterious milk sickness claimed many lives in the American Midwest. Dr. Anna Pierce Hobbs Bixby is largely credited with discovering its link to white snakeroot. An elderly friend of Dr. Bixby's, a Shawnee woman whose name is lost to history, described the plant's properties, and with a little testing, Dr. Bixby confirmed that the illness came from dairy or meat from animals who had grazed on white snakeroot. She petitioned to eradicate the plant in 1834. Unfortunately, no one heeded her warning. Eventually, it was figured out again by a farmer in 1967.

Snapdragon

PRESUMPTION

An old German superstition suggests preparing a bouquet of snapdragon, black cumin, and blue marjoram, combined with a right shirtsleeve and a left stocking, to protect babies from an evil child-snatcher. The tradition links to the folktale of Nickert, the small gray water dweller who switched unbaptized babies for his own, big-headed children.

Sneezewort

FREEDOM

Also known as **Fair-Maid-of-France**. The petite daisy-like flowers of the sneezewort grow widely across Europe, as well as some spots across North America. Leaves from this plant were added to snuff recipes. It was believed that sneezewort would not only make you sneeze but cause nosebleeds as well. Seventeenth-century English herbalist Nicholas Culpeper recommended using the plant to relieve congestion.

Snowdrop

HOPE

One of the first to bloom when the weather warms, the snowdrop is a comforting harbinger of spring. The flowers contain an active substance known as galantamine, which modern medicine uses to help treat the neurological and muscular symptoms of diseases such as polio and Alzheimer's.

Solomon's Seal

SECRET

Solomon's seal was named after the Hebrew king from the first century BCE. Legend says that he was bestowed with a magical signet ring that gave him the power to command animals and demons. The flat top of the metal ring featured a raised decorative hexagram—a motif that in time became known as the Star of David. This ring was used as a personal seal, stamping his signature insignia onto documents or tablets. When the rootstalk of the plant Solomon's seal is cut, it scars in a way that resembles the king's seal.

SOLOMON'S SEAL

SNEEZEWORT

Sorrel

PARENTAL AFFECTION

Also known as **Spinach Dock**.

With reddish-purple flower spikes, garden sorrel is mostly cultivated as an edible vegetable. It is used in stews from Nigeria to eastern Europe. Ashkenazi Jews make a soup often referred to as green borscht. It has also long been used as a healing herbal wash to soothe chickenpox sores.

Wild Sorrel
Wit ill timed

Southernwood

BANTERING

To avoid dozing off during long sermons, churchgoers wore sprigs of camphor-scented southernwood. The feathery green leaves were also strewn in prisons in the hopes that it would stop the spread of disease. Judges were known to carry the herb when they went to court so as to not contract typhoid from the prisoners. While southernwood is rarely used medicinally these days, the essential oil is still used as an aromatic herbal tonic by some to remain alert during social occasions.

SNOWDROP

SOUTHERNWOOD

SORREL

Spiderwort

ESTEEM, NOT LOVE

This flowering plant is named spiderwort
because it has the look of many legs. An old
English word, *wort* simply means "plant."
A common name for this invasive plant is
wandering Jew, which stems from an anti-
Semitic character in thirteenth-century
folklore. An evil tradesman, the wandering
Jew is punished to roam for all eternity. The
"Eternal Jew" archetype was rehashed in
Nazi propaganda. The 1940 film *Der ewige
Jude* was presented as a documentary,
portraying this caricature of Jewish people
as parasitic and worthy of extermination.

Virginia Spiderwort
Momentary happiness

Spindle

YOUR CHARMS ARE ENGRAVED
ON MY HEART

The hardwood of this tree was used
to make spindles for turning wool. In
the fairy tale *Sleeping Beauty*, a young
princess pricks her finger on a spindle. A
spinning wheel can be seen as a symbol
for a woman's life cycle. The occupation of
spinning was typically reserved for young
unmarried women. Then after years serving
as a mother and wife, a woman becomes
a wise old crone, who once again will pick
up the practice. The lipstick-pink berries
hold little orange fruit that contain alkaloids,
theobromine, and caffeine, which if
consumed may induce a Sleeping Beauty–
type coma.

SPIDERWORT

SPRUCE

ST. JOHN'S
WORT

SPINDLE

Spruce

HOPE IN ADVERSITY

Native American nations, including the Inuit, Cree, and Hanaksiala, chewed wads of spruce sap for both its medicinal use and its pleasing woodsy flavor. Colonists learned of this treat, and in 1848 "State of Maine Pure Spruce Gum" was the first commercially available gum. Although there are other ancient chewing traditions from around the world, this series of events is what eventually led to the development of the gum we are familiar with today.

Black Spruce
Pity

Norway Spruce
Farewell

St. John's Wort

SUPERSTITION

St. John's wort was traditionally gathered in England for rituals and festivities on St. John's Day (June 24). Decked with crowns of St. John's wort and verbena, young people would dance around a bonfire. Praying to the saint for a better year to come, they would throw flowers into the flames. In France and Germany, the flower was hung above doors to repel evil spirits from entering their homes.

Star of Bethlehem

PURITY

Inspired by homeopathy in the 1930s,
Dr. Edward Bach claimed that the dew
on flower petals held specific healing
properties. Believing the flowers contained
a vibrational nature, he composed tinctures
intuitively, based on a perceived psychic
connection to plants. Bach recommended
a star of Bethlehem tincture for folks
who witnessed or endured a shocking or
traumatic event.

Statice

SYMPATHY

Also known as **Sea Lavender, Limonium**.
The papery statice flowers are favored
in dried arrangements, as the bloom's
color and texture maintain vibrancy and
freshness. One Victorian trend was to
keep compositions of dried botanicals in
a bell jar or other glass display. No longer
living, these preserved plants conjured the
passage from life into death.

Stephanotis

WILL YOU ACCOMPANY ME TO THE EAST?

Also known as **Hawaiian Wedding Flower,
Madagascar Jasmine**. The fragrant
Stephanotis of Madagascar is a popular
addition to bridal bouquets. The white
blooms conjure thoughts of marital bliss as
well as happy travels. The name is derived
from the Greek word meaning "fit for a
crown." Brides in ancient Greece wore
special crowns called *stephane*.

STATICE

STINGING
NETTLE

STAR OF
BETHLEHEM

STOCK

Stinging Nettle

YOU ARE SPITEFUL

The tiny hairs on nettles impale human skin, producing a stinging pain, inflamed redness, and irritation. In the seventeenth and eighteenth century, some Europeans, including philosopher John Locke, considered flogging with stinging nettles a potential cure for palsy or paralysis. This type of treatment was used as a punishment for criminals in Ecuador and as a way to punish children in England, Russia, India, and elsewhere around the world.

Stock

LASTING BEAUTY

Also known as *Gillyflower*.

A botanical relative of the cabbage, stock is an edible flower. With frilly florets growing up slender stems, stock was incredibly popular in Saxony during the sixteenth century for its beauty and clove-like scent. The government gave each village a specific color of stock to breed.

Red Stock
Boredom

Ten-Week Stock
Promptness

STEPHANOTIS

Straw

UNION

In 922 CE, King Charles the Simple was confronted by powerful noblemen who declared him incapable. To make it clear that they would no longer submit to his authority, Frankish noblemen approached the throne and broke handfuls of straw in front of the king, throwing the debris to the ground. All contracts between the parties henceforth became null and void.

Broken Straw
Rupture of contract

Strawberry Blossom

PERFECT GOODNESS

The sweet strawberry resembles the human heart, so it is not surprising that many Native American languages have a name for the fruit that translates to something like "heart berry." It is an Ojibwe tradition that a young woman must abstain from strawberries and other berries for one year after she begins menstruating. During this time, she learns about womanhood from her grandmothers and gathers berries to share with everyone at the end of her fast.

STRAWBERRY TREE

STRAW

STRAWBERRY BLOSSOM

SUMAC

Strawberry Tree

ESTEEM AND LOVE

Also known as **Arbutus**. The warty red and yellow bounty of the strawberry tree is unrelated to the common berries of the same name. Left to ripen, the fruit begins to ferment while still hanging on the branches. Bears have been known to enjoy getting drunk on this boozy snack. The coat of arms of Madrid features a bear standing next to a *madroño* tree, as they are known in Spanish. This imagery appears throughout the city on taxis, manhole covers, and elsewhere. There is even a statue of the bear eating the fruit located in the city center. The American cousin to this tree is the Pacific madrone.

Sumac

SPLENDOR

The tart fruit known as drupes is ground into a spice that is used in za'atar, the popular Middle Eastern spice blend. Traditionally, the soft Morocco leather used for book bindings and gloves was tanned with sumac. The Lenape people of the Northeastern Woodlands of the Americas smoked pipes filled with a specific blend of tobacco and roasted sumac leaves. Their name for this plant, *Kelelenikanakw*, means "mixture tree."

Sunflower

FALSE RICHES

See page 222.
Native to North and South Americas, the sunflower has been cultivated as a food source for about three thousand years. The petals, leaves, and seeds can all be enjoyed for their nutritional value. Zuni healers would chew on this flower before sucking the venom out of a snakebite. It is also used as a healing poultice for rattlesnake bites.

Dwarf Sunflower
Your devout admirer

Sweet Pea

DELICATE PLEASURES

Sweet peas are beloved for their petals that curl in a gentle, dainty way. At one time this species was barely noticed, but crossbreeding during the Victorian era produced new sensational varieties, and it has been extremely popular ever since. Folklore suggests that planting sweet peas before the sun rises on St. Patrick's Day will not only bring luck your way but will also help the sweet-smelling flowers grow abundantly.

SUNFLOWER

SWEET PEA

Sweet William

GALLANTRY

Also known as **Bearded Pink**. It is not known to which William sweet William refers, although there is speculation—including the Bard, William Shakespeare himself. It is a unique flower in that it has been given a masculine name. In 1717, the first-ever artificial floral hybrid was a cross between a sweet William and a carnation.

Sycamore

CURIOSITY

In a biblical tale from the New Testament, Jesus is visiting the town of Jericho, and a crowd gathers to see him. Zacchaeus, a tax collector who happened to be quite short, climbed up a sycamore fig tree so he could catch a glimpse of the Messiah. Jesus spotted him up in the tree and addressed him by name.

SWEET WILLIAM

SYCAMORE

221 \ FLOWERS AND THEIR MEANINGS

Sunflower

FALSE RICHES

See page 220

The oil derived from the sunflower seed is not only used for edible consumption. It also has many industrial applications, including use in various varnishes, paints, and sustainable plastics. Surprisingly, sunflower oil contains almost as much energy as diesel fuel. Biodiesel made from this plant can be used as an alternate energy source. Flowers transform sunlight into chemical energy, and as the sunflower matures, it turns—with a proud posture—toward the sun to absorb its solar rays. Once the sunflower is in full bloom, it remains facing east to greet the rising sun.

One of the by-products of sunflower oil extraction is a tremendous volume of empty flower husks. Once the seeds are removed, these shells are sometimes compressed into pellets. These pill-shaped bits of raw botanical material are used as an energy source for many applications, from fueling furnace heating systems to even running power plants in the United Kingdom and Poland. Although the sunflower can be used as a biofuel, the large-scale farming necessary to effectively manufacture this powerful "fuel" creates many environmental concerns. The ecological impact and potential benefits are still being studied by scientists.

In addition to biofuel, the roots and stems of the sunflower offer another eco-friendly application. The flower's hollow stalks are sturdy enough to make a variety of flotation devices. Special rafts made of these stems were used in the environmental disaster relief in Chernobyl in the 1980s. The roots draw in contaminants from water and, in this case, removed up to 95 percent of the radioactive waste. For this reason, the flower has become a global emblem of nuclear disarmament.

T

Tamarisk

CRIME

Criminals in ancient Rome were apparently marked with a wreath of slim branches of tamarisk on their head. In the Qur'an, the people of Saba were punished for their lack of obedience to Allah. Their once-plentiful gardens could suddenly grow only bitter, bad fruit, tamarisk, and a few sparse lote trees.

Tansy

I DECLARE WAR AGAINST YOU

This potent and bitter flower was used as an abortifacient in the Middle Ages. It was also used as a treatment for intestinal worms, to repel flies, as a facial cleanser, and even worn in shoes to prevent malaria. To give a stalk of wild tansy is considered a bold insult.

Thistle

AUSTERITY

Scottish legend describes a cruel invasion of Danes in the fifteenth century. Even though it was considered "unwarlike" to attack at night, the Danish invaders crept into an encampment of sleeping Scots. Tiptoeing barefoot under the cloak of darkness, the soldiers cried out when they stepped on sharp thistles, waking the slumbering men. Emblematic of protection and bravery, the thistle is the Scottish national flower.

Thorns

SEVERITY

Well known in many languages, the proverb "Every rose has its thorn" has an unknown origin. Even something as beautiful as a rose is not without flaws. Related sayings include the Persian "He who wants a rose must respect the thorn" and the Swedish "If you are among the roses, your friends will look for you among the thorns."

Evergreen Thorns
Solace in adversity

THORNS

TANSY

TAMARISK

THISTLE

Thyme

ACTIVITY

In the Middle Ages, ladies would stitch the image of a bee hovering over a sprig of thyme on scarves to present to their knights. One poetic interpretation of this imagery is "However far away you may 'bee,' and whatever 'thyme' passes, I will 'bee' here, waiting and faithful." A courting tradition from that era was the offering of a sprig of fragrant thyme, which was a coy way to express intent of marriage. If the herb was accepted, the reply was understood: *I am interested. Go talk to my parents.*

Wild Thyme
Thoughtlessness

Trillium

MODEST BEAUTY

Considered a sacred female herb, many cultures have used trillium root to assist with childbirth and other women's health issues. The trio of petals that all trilliums have are linked to the three expected stages of a woman's life: maiden, mother, and crone.

TUBEROSE

THYME

TRUMPET VINE

TULIP

TRILLIUM

Trumpet Vine

SEPARATION

The trumpet vine has been classified and reclassified throughout the centuries as the science of taxonomy became more sophisticated. Virginia settlers first identified the flower as a jasmine, then a honeysuckle. Later it was believed to be part of the bellflower family and then associated with the *Apocynum* (dogbane) genus and *Bignonia* genus. In 1867, it was ultimately revised and reclassified as part of the *Campsis* genus, which includes two species of flowering climbers that have aerial roots.

Tuberose

DANGEROUS PLEASURES

Marie Antoinette wore a perfume called *sillage de la reine* that contained tuberose, orange blossom, sandalwood, jasmine, iris, and cedar. The word *sillage* translates as "the degree to which a perfume lingers in the air when worn." A powerful fragrance, it was suggested that tuberose should be experienced only at a distance, at night, lest the perfume overwhelm and kill you.

Tulip

DECLARATION OF LOVE

See page 228.
An important part of the country's botanical history and culture, the elegant tulip is proudly the national flower of Turkey. A vulgar Turkish insult is to call someone an "ass tulip," akin to a douchebag.

Striped Tulip
Beautiful eyes

Yellow Tulip
Hopeless love

Tulip

DECLARATION OF LOVE

See page 227

Tulips were first cultivated by Sultan Suleiman the Magnificent sometime around 1050 CE in Istanbul. The flowers were grown in traditional walled-off Persian gardens called *pairi-daēza*, an ancient Iranian term for what is now known as paradise gardens.

Derived from the Latin word *tulipa*, meaning "turban," "gauze," or "muslin," the name was chosen to describe the flower's resemblance to a turban. The flowers came in various vividly saturated hues and were considered an exotic and coveted luxury item in Europe. Some blooms were streaked with multiple colors (which botanists now know is caused by a virus spread by aphids). This flame-like effect stunned and captivated Europeans; botanists attempted to cultivate an even wider variety of multicolored flowers, even grafting healthy bulbs to "broken" ones.

These highly coveted bulbs sparked the seventeenth-century frenzy known as Tulipomania. At the time, the exoticized tulip's rare bulbs sold for thousands of florins. The Dutch bought and sold bulbs on mere speculation, and the market based on tulip futures exploded. People gambled on the delusional idea that one particular bulb would be so unique in its striping that they would have complete control of the future of that particular species. People traded their possessions for the flowers, thinking them a safe bet to acquire greater wealth. Some paid the equivalent of a nice canal house—tenfold a skilled craftsman's yearly income—for one bulb from the Ottoman Empire.

The bubble popped. Tulipomania lasted only a year. By 1637, the value of a bulb was a mere 5 percent of the previously soaring prices. The collapse left many people in serious financial ruin. It is believed to have been the first recorded speculative bubble burst.

One factor that may have influenced the crash was a concurrent outbreak of the bubonic plague. The pandemic increased risk-taking behaviors in some people, who paid outrageous prices for tulips they would never be able to resell at a profit. Despite it all, tulips remain a big export for the Netherlands, where about two billion tulips are produced annually. This accounts for roughly 90 percent of all tulips worldwide.

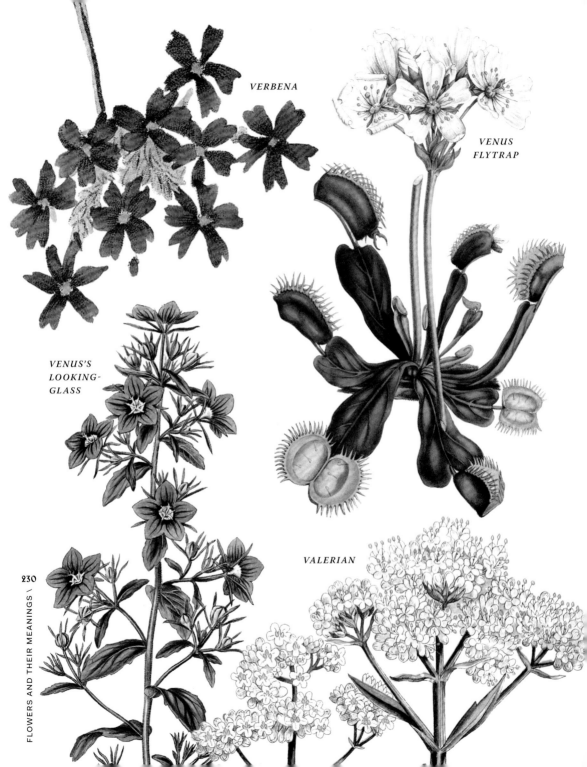

VERBENA

VENUS
FLYTRAP

VENUS'S
LOOKING-
GLASS

VALERIAN

V

Valerian

AN ACCOMMODATING
DISPOSITION

A scrambling plant, old ruins provide the perfect textured surfaces for valerian to climb and grow on. As an herbal remedy, it has been used to relax anxious humans and dogs. Cats love to roll around in this plant, gnawing and sniffing the flowers, which some say smell like dirty socks. As a result, the felines get a little euphoric on this mild intoxicant. They are likely responding to the valeric acid, which is also found in the sex pheromones released in the urine of female cats.

Venus Flytrap

DECEIT

This infamously carnivorous plant seduces bugs with its sweet nectar. When prey touches the tiny trigger hairs on the inner surface of the plant, the "trap" suddenly closes. The more the prey moves, the tighter the flytrap's grip gets. Over the course of a week, the Venus flytrap releases digestive juices to drown the insect and then slowly consume it. A single plant might eat only a few times in its life. Because they were often found growing near sites where meteors had landed, some people thought the Venus flytrap was from outer space.

Venus's Looking-Glass

FLATTERY

The lovely purple petals of this ornamental flower abruptly close as soon as the sky clouds or the sun sets. Many believe that the name was inspired by the seeds, which are so shiny that they reflect the beauty of the flower.

Verbena

SENSIBILITY

Also known as **Vervain**. Verbena has been connected to the divine for centuries. Christian legend tells us that the herb was used to staunch the wounds of Jesus after he was removed from the cross. The ancient Egyptians knew this plant as "tears of Isis" and the Greeks referred to it as "Hera's tears." Believing that verbena could make peace between enemies, Greek ambassadors would wear a sprig when venturing to make a treaty.

Pink Verbena
Family union

Scarlet Verbena
Unity against evil

White Verbena
Pray for me

Veronica

FIDELITY

Also known as **Germander Speedwell, Bird's Eye Speedwell, Cat Eyes**. Once plucked from the stem, veronica blossoms wilt right away. This characteristic inspired the tongue-in-cheek German name for this flower, *Männertreu*, which translates to "men's faithfulness." In the eighteenth century, veronica was used to make tea and was believed to be a cure for gout. It was so popular that the plant nearly became extinct in London.

Veronica spicata
Resemblance

VINE

Viburnum

I DIE IF NEGLECTED

Also known as **Snowball, Guelder Rose**. Viburnum features distinct white globular flower heads and bright red berries. The fruit is often depicted in Ukrainian embroidery, poetry, and folk songs, as Slavic paganism associates this plant with the birth of the universe. The berries are referred to as "the fire trinity," representing homeland, blood, and family roots.

Snowball Blossoms
Winter of age

232

VIBURNUM

VERONICA

VIOLET

Vine

INTOXICATION

Vines encompass a wide variety of plants with tendril-like stems that trail or climb. In many old English texts, the word *vine* is used for one of the most essential vines and the source of wine: the grapevine. The Scythian philosopher Anacharsis of the sixth century BCE once said, "Vine produces three kinds of fruit—intoxication, debauchery, and repentance."

Violet

MODESTY

See page 234.
When Napoleon Bonaparte abdicated the throne in 1814, he proclaimed that although he was leaving France in exile, he would return with the violets—meaning in the springtime, when his favorite flowers were in bloom. Wearing this flower became a way to signify support for him. The covert question "Are you fond of the violet?" was a method of testing political affiliations. To knowingly answer with *"Eh! Bien!"* (Ah! Well!) revealed a shared understanding. This winking exchange would be confirmed with the final statement "It will reappear in spring."

Blue Violet
Faithfulness

Double Violet
Reciprocal friendship

White Violet
Candor

Yellow Violet
Rural happiness

Violet

MODESTY

See page 233

In the mid-nineteenth century, a corsage of fragrant *Viola odorata* was an extremely popular fashion accessory. The trend developed in France, then England, and spread through central and eastern Europe and eventually to North America. By the 1880s, Rhinebeck, New York, had established itself as the violet capital of the world. While the violet, which happened to be Queen Victoria's favorite flower, is a delightfully attractive blossom, it is adored mostly for its intoxicating scent. During the nineteenth century, violets were used to scent soaps and tooth powder and to flavor baked goods, jellies, and candies. Stationery and inks scented with violets were so fashionable that postal workers complained of their sacks of letters reeking of perfume.

Augustin Francisco Reyes was an internationally recognized Cuban perfumer. When he fled Castro's revolution in 1960, everything had to be left behind, although he did manage to bring a few handwritten pages of fragrance formulas on his journey to Miami. The family relaunched and renamed the company's signature scent Royal Violets. The cologne, which is specifically designed for babies, is a regional tradition that is still going strong. The fragrance for infants is readily available in pharmacies in Miami.

For a flower known for its smell, violets strangely can only be sensed for one sniff at a time. Due to the ionones present, smell receptors turn off after a few seconds. Once the brain has a little bit of time to reboot, it is able to detect the scent again.

A great many ladies have developed a passion for chewing violets. They depart a delicious fragrance to the breath, and even at a cent a piece are cheap for this purpose. . . . It is interesting to know that many belles have a fancy for thrusting bunches of fresh violets in mysterious places about their corsets, professing to believe that the crushed flowers exhale a more delicately delicious perfume than any of the myriad scented stuffs that they can buy in bottles. And the florists encourage the fashion enthusiastically.

—New York Times, *1877*

W

Wallflower

FIDELITY IN MISFORTUNE

The wallflower famously grows from the silty mortar between the bricks and stones of ruinous walls of ancient castles, abbeys, turrets, and cottages. Although this fragrant and colorful plant is a shrub that thrives in a variety of arid conditions, such as flowerpots or garden borders, the image of this plant clinging to a wall is conjured when an introvert sits off to the side at a school dance.

Walnut

STRATAGEM

In 1597, during the Franco-Spanish War, the French city of Amiens was sieged by Spaniards disguised as country folk. In order to storm the city gates, the Spaniards released a humongous supply of walnuts, pretending it was an accident. Amid the pandemonium, they were able to storm the city. To this day, "Walnut Eaters" is a moniker bestowed on the people of Amiens.

Water Lily

PURITY OF HEART

In 1998, the discovery of a 125-million-year-old fossilized plant in northeastern China made botanical waves. Identified as *Archaefructus sinensis* at the time of its discovery, the plant became the oldest-known flowering plant in the world. Its closest living relation is likely the water lily. According to Egyptian myth, the sacred blue water lily appeared in dark waters, the petals unfurling to reveal the young Nefertum, god of perfume, sitting in the flower's golden heart.

Water Willow

FREEDOM

Despite its name, the water willow is not related to willow trees. An aquatic-flowering plant, the water willow grows tall and blossoms well above the surface of the water. The submerged portion of the plant provides a habitat for small fish. Predator fish, such as largemouth bass, linger nearby, waiting for their chance to catch a meal. Meanwhile, humans cast a line in the same location, hoping to reel in hungry bass.

WALLFLOWER

WATER
WILLOW

WALNUT

Watermelon Blossom

BULKINESS

The juicy red flesh of the watermelon is a delicious and refreshing treat, but some tales of the watermelon are surprisingly sinister. The Roma people of the Balkans have a folkloric warning: If you keep a watermelon too long, it may turn into a watermelon vampire. A drop of blood on the rind of the fruit is a signal that the melon's transformation is about to begin.

Wheat

PROSPERITY

Nineteenth-century tombstones often feature carvings of symbolic botanical imagery. A decorative sheaf of wheat was carved onto gravestones to honor someone who died in old age. The symbol represented harvest time—having lived a long and prosperous life, it was time for these elders to meet the Grim Reaper (often depicted with a scythe), who would take them away.

WILLOW

WATERMELON BLOSSOM

WHEAT

WINTER CHERRY

Willow

FORSAKEN

The weeping willow may droop in a mournful posture, but no matter how many branches you cut from the tree, it continues to flourish. For thousands of years, an extract from willow bark has been administered as a tea to treat fever, pain, and inflammation. Evidence of this medicinal use appears in Sumerian clay tablets and Egyptian papyrus. This willow extract is better known today as ASA, or acetylsalicylic acid, the active ingredient in aspirin. In the nineteenth century, a French chemist named Charles Frédéric Gerhardt developed a method to synthetically produce the acid.

Basket Willow
Frankness

Weeping Willow
Mourning

Winter Cherry

DECEPTION

Also known as **Chinese Lantern, Bladder Cherry**. The edible fruit of the winter cherry is revealed when its papery orange husk—which looks like a lantern—disintegrates, leaving only netted skeletal remains. The winter cherry has been celebrated as a curative and sacred herb by many cultures. In Japan, this plant is known as *hozuki* and is given as an offering to guide the souls of the dead.

Wisteria

WELCOME, FAIR STRANGER

Tea has been an integral part of Chinese culture for thousands of years. In the mid-1800s, as afternoon tea became popular in Britain, the British East India Company sent a spy to steal trade secrets from China. Foreigners were prohibited from entering China's interior, but wearing a Mandarin disguise, botanist Robert Fortune snuck in and gained access to horticultural-growing techniques and tea-processing methods. He smuggled a variety of seeds, cuttings of premium green and black tea plants, and samples of yellow rose, winter jasmine, and wisteria. Many botanical histories attribute the "discovery" of these flowers to Fortune.

Witch Hazel

A SPELL

Witch hazel branches have long been used as divining rods in the search for underground water sources. Nine-thousand-year-old pictographs found in the Tassili-n-Ajjer caves in Libya depict people watching a dowser, the person who holds the forked branch. The practice involves pacing until the stick swivels toward the ground. Pressed, boiled, and steamed, this plant is used as a topical astringent and anti-inflammatory treatment.

WOOD SORREL

WISTERIA

WITCH HAZEL

WOOD SORREL

Wood Sorrel

JOY

Also known as **Oxalis,** *False Shamrock*. Some species of this genus are easily mistaken for clover. The oxalic acid found in this plant is responsible for its mildly sour flavor. The Ka'igwu (Kiowa) people of the American Great Plains traditionally chewed these leaves to keep themselves hydrated on long trips. A cold wood sorrel tea was used by the Anigiduwagi (Cherokee) to stop vomiting. It was also used as an aphrodisiac by the Algonquins.

Wormwood

ABSENCE

Wormwood is one of the herbs used to produce the hallucinogenic alcohol known as absinthe. The plant contains thujone, high concentrations of which can cause seizures and death. Any amount of thujone is banned in the United States.

WORMWOOD

241 \ FLOWERS AND THEIR MEANINGS

Y

Yarrow

WAR

Yarrow's genus name, *Achillea*, is a reference to the mythical figure of Achilles, who carried reserves of the blossom onto the battlefield to treat his army. Yarrow is known for its blood-clotting properties and is used as a poultice for wounds.

Yew

SORROW

Yew trees are believed to live as long as two thousand years, but they hollow out as they age, making it difficult to confirm. Ancient Roman invaders held church services under yew trees in order to appeal to the nature-loving pagans. To this day, these trees, which were associated with magic, are found alongside many churches across England.

YARROW

YEW

Z

Zephyrlily

EXPECTATION

Zephyr comes from the Greek *zephyranthes*, meaning "flowers of the west wind." This flower has been used as an herbal treatment for a variety of ailments around the world, including tumors in Peru, breast cancer in China, and diabetes in some parts of Africa.

Zinnia

THOUGHTS OF ABSENT FRIENDS

A garden favorite, this flower appears in a wide range of bright, saturated hues. The zinnia is a symbol of wisdom for the Pueblo people of the American Southwest. For this reason, the edible flower was fed to children with the wish that they grow to be intelligent and well spoken.

ZINNIA

Mood Index

ASPIRATIONS & GRATITUDE

A wish / *Foxglove*
Ambition / *Mountain Laurel,
     Dark-Colored Hollyhock*
Aspiring / *Mountain Pink*
Confidence / *Hepatica, Lilac Primrose*
Desire for riches / *Kingcup Marigold*
Dreams / *Osmunda*
Encouragement / *Goldenrod, Deep Pink Rose*
Fame / *Angel's Trumpet*
Female ambition / *White Hollyhock*
Genius / *Plane*
Gratitude / *White Bellflower*
I surmount all difficulties / *Mistletoe*
Inspiration / *Angelica*
My gratitude exceeds your care /
     Dahlias (a bunch)
Success crowns your wishes / *Coronilla*
Talent / *White Pink*
Thankfulness / *Agrimony*
Victory / *Palm*
Wit / *Ragged-Robin*
Worth beyond beauty / *Sweet Alyssum*

CHARACTER TRAITS

Amiability / *Jasmine*
**An accommodating
     disposition** / *Valerian*
Audacity / *Larch*
Boldness / *Pink*
Capricious beauty /
     *Lady's Slipper Orchid,
     Musk Rose*
Desire to please /
     Daphne Mezereum
Energy in adversity /
     Chamomile
Fickleness / *Pink Delphinium*
Gallantry / *Sweet William*
Honesty / *Money Plant*

Innocence / *Daisy*
Instability / *Dahlia*
Modesty / *Violet*
Rudeness / *Clotbur*
Sensitiveness / *Mimosa*
Sourness of temper / *Barberry*
Strength / *Cedar, Fennel*
Temperance / *Azalea*
Transient beauty /
     Night-Blooming Cereus

COMMITMENT

Be mine / *Four-leaf Clover*
Bonds of love / *Honeysuckle*
Chastity / *Orange Blossom, Cinnamon*
Conjugal love / *Linden*
Discretion / *Maidenhair Fern*
Faithfulness / *Blue Violet*
Fidelity / *Veronica*
Fidelity in love / *Lemon Blossoms*
I attach myself to you / *Indian
     Jasmine, Red Morning Glory*
Indiscretion / *Almond, Cattail, Feathery Reeds*
Infidelity / *Yellow Rose*
Marriage / *Ivy*
Refusal / *Striped Pink, Striped Carnation*
Rupture of contract / *Broken Straw*
Unfortunate attachment / *Scabiosa*
Unity / *Red and White Roses (together)*
You have no claim / *Pasque Flower*

COMPLIMENTS & CHEER

Always cheerful / *Coreopsis*
Beautiful eyes / *Striped Tulip*
Brilliant complexion / *Damask Rose*
Cheerfulness under adversity /
     Chrysanthemum
Delicate beauty / *Hibiscus*
Elegance / *Rose Acacia*
Gaiety / *Butterfly Orchid*
Her smile, the soul of witchery /
     Wild Blue Lupine
I am dazzled by your charms / *Ranunculus*

Joy / *Wood Sorrel*

Magnificent beauty / *Calla Lily*

Mature charms / *Cattleya Orchid*

Pensive beauty / *Laburnum*

Perfection of female loveliness / *Justicia*

Return of happiness / *Lily of the Valley*

Sun-beaming eyes / *Maltese Cross*

Thou art all that is lovely / *Austrian Rose*

Transport of joy / *Gardenia*

Worth beyond beauty / *Sweet Alyssum*

You are rich in attractions / *Garden Ranunculus*

FLIRTATION & SENSUALITY

Ardor / *Arum*

Blushes / *Marjoram*

Coquetry / *Daylily*

Dangerous pleasures / *Tuberose*

Delicate pleasures / *Sweet Pea*

Excess of beauty hath bewitched me / *Feathered Hyacinth*

Fires of the heart / *Red-and-White Rose*

First emotions of love / *Lilac*

First language of love / *Yellow Jasmine*

First sigh of love / *Greater Celandine*

Flirtation / *Variegated Poppy*

I am your captive / *Peach Blossom*

Passion / *White Fraxinella*

Pleasure and pain / *Dog Rose*

Sensuality / *Spanish Jasmine*

Sweets to the sweet / *Daphne odora*

Voluptuousness / *Moss Rose*

Voraciousness / *Lupine*

You are the queen of coquettes / *Dame's Rocket*

Your hand for the next dance / *Ivy Geranium*

INSULTS & LOATHING

Avarice / *Scarlet Auricula*

Death preferable to loss of innocence / *White Rose (dried)*

Deceitful charms / *Datura*

Disappointed expectation / *Fish Geranium*

Disgust / *Frog Orchid*

Distrust / *Lavender*

Flee away! / *Pennyroyal*

Hatred / *Basil*

I change but in death / *Bay Leaf*

I declare against you / *Belvedere*

I die if neglected / *Viburnum*

I shall die tomorrow / *Gum Cistus*

I will never beg / *Rose Leaf*

I will not survive you / *Black Mulberry*

Ill nature / *Crabapple Blossom*

Let me go / *Butterfly Weed*

Misanthropy / *Fuller's Teasel*

Scandal / *Hellebore, Bicolor Rose*

Stupidity / *Scarlet Geranium*

Thy frown will kill me / *Currant*

Touch me not / *Red Impatiens, Burdock*

You are spiteful / *Stinging Nettle*

You will cause my death / *Hemlock*

Your whims are quite unbearable / *Bee Balm*

LOVE & FRIENDSHIP

Affection / *Mossy Saxifrage, Morning Glory*

Consumed by love / *Rose of Sharon*

Declaration of love / *Tulip*

Early friendship / *Blue Periwinkle*

Esteem and love / *Strawberry Tree*

Forget me not / *Forget-Me-Not, Yellow-and-Purple Mixed Pansy*

Friendship / *Acacia*

Happy love / *Bridal Rose*

If you love me, you will find it out / *Maiden Blush Rose*

Love / *Myrtle, Red Rose*

Love at first sight / *Coreopsis arkansa*
Love returned / *Ragweed*
Love sweet and secret / *Honey Flower*
Pure and ardent love / *Red Carnation, Red Pink*
Reciprocal friendship / *Double Violet*
Secret love / *Yellow Acacia*
True friendship / *Oak-Leaved Geranium*
Unchanging friendship / *Arborvitae*
You occupy my thoughts / *Purple Pansy*
Your charms are engraved on my heart / *Spindle*

SADNESS & CONDOLENCES; APOLOGIES

Affection beyond the grave / *Locust*
Consolation / *Poppy*
Cure for heartache / *Cranberry Blossom*
Extinguishing hopes / *Blue Bindweed*
Grief / *Aloe, Harebell, Marigold*
Hopeless love / *Yellow Tulip*
I am sorry / *Purple Hyacinth*
I love you best when you are sad / *Gentian*
Melancholy spirit / *Sad Geranium*
Mourning / *Weeping Willow*
My heart bleeds for you / *Camellia japonica*
My regrets follow you to the grave / *Asphodel*
Pleasures of memory / *White Periwinkle*
Remembrance / *Rosemary*
Remorse / *Raspberry Blossom*
Slighted love / *Yellow Chrysanthemum*
Sorrowful remembrance / *Adonis*
Sympathy / *Statice*
Tears / *Helenium*
Tender recollections / *Periwinkle*
Thoughts of absent friends / *Zinnia*
Widowhood / *Mourning Bride (Sweet Scabiosa)*
Your presence softens my pain / *Milkvetch*

SPIRITUALITY

A spell / *Witch Hazel*
Confidence in heaven / *Flowering Reeds*
Pray for me / *White Verbena*
Religious superstition / *Aloe, Passion Flower*
Rustic oracle / *Dandelion*
Secret / *Solomon's Seal*
Silence / *White Rose, Belladonna*
Sorcery / *Enchanter's Nightshade*
Spiritual beauty / *Cherry Blossom*
Superstition / *St. John's Wort*
Truth / *Bittersweet Nightshade, White Chrysanthemum*
Unity against evil / *Scarlet Verbena*
You are my divinity / *Shooting Star*

STATE OF MIND

Anxious and trembling / *Red Columbine*
Boredom / *Red Stock*
Bravery / *Oak Leaves*
Calm repose / *Buckbean*
Curiosity / *Sycamore*
Freedom / *Sneezewort, Water Willow*
Hope / *Almond Blossom, Hawthorn, Snowdrop*
Hope in adversity / *Spruce*
Impatience / *Impatiens*
Intoxication / *Vine*
Patience / *Ox-Eye Daisy, Galium*
Peace / *Olive Branch*
Resolved to win / *Purple Columbine*
Sleep. My bane, my antidote / *White Poppy*
Thoughts / *Pansy*

ACKNOWLEDGMENTS

About the Author

Karen Azoulay is a visual artist and author. She lives in Brooklyn, New York.

THE OPPORTUNITY TO WRITE and share this book has me filled with so much gratitude. Many people helped along the way, and I share a deep heartfelt thanks to you all.

Gillian MacKenzie made this adventure less intimidating with her enthusiasm, encouragement, and support. She also found the perfect home for *Flowers and Their Meanings*.

Sara Neville saw the potential in this publication and walked alongside me on this journey. Her bright editorial guidance and focus have been a vital part of shaping this book. Lise Sukhu and Danielle Deschenes provided the beautiful design that brings these pages together. Patricia Shaw, Jessica Heim, Chloe Aryeh, and everyone at Clarkson Potter who had a hand in bringing this project to fruition—thank you! It is an incredible privilege to collaborate with such a talented team.

Jean-Guillaume Buckel, Sedona Cohen, Mikaela Dery, Cliff Frost, Simone Rose Edgar Holmes, Mustafa Önder, Chrysanne Stathacos, Katja von Schuttenbach, and Satoshi Tsuchiyama each assisted with my research in some way, translated a text, or answered cultural questions.

Jordan Merica, Valerie Fridland, and Richard McCracken provided invaluable insights in their areas of expertise. Likewise, botanist Clarice Guan was a crucial collaborator, clarifying my plant facts.

Many librarians and archivists helped point me in the right direction, including Stephen Sinon at the New York Botanical Garden and Kathy Crosby at Brooklyn Botanic Garden.

Carl Williamson came up with the title *Flowers and Their Meanings*.

Sedona Cohen, Sheryl Cook, Maritza Myrthil, Arly Scott, Alexander Paris, and Amy Khoshbin modeled their gorgeous features for the photography. Lorie Reilly was an integral part of the photo shoots capturing these images.

Bianca Beck, Jude Broughan, Michael Cobb, Rachel Domm, Sophia Peer, and Margaret Stevens gave valuable feedback time and time again.

To all of my supportive friends and family cheering me on . . . I simply couldn't have done it without you.

When I revealed my pie-in-the-sky idea for this book to Kate Bolick, she responded with such enthusiastic encouragement, I was sparked into motion. Her wise advice and support during this process saved me countless times. That she generously lent her beautiful words for the foreword is the cherry on top.

George McCracken's unwavering steadiness anchored me in my moments of doubt. His support, patience, and encouragement have been a huge contribution to this project (and my sanity). Among other sweet gestures that have filled my heart with happiness, he has proven that the romance of flowers is real.

For Further Reading

Botanical Folk Tales of Britain and Ireland, by Lisa Schneidau, 2018

Botanical Shakespeare, by Gerit Quealy and Sumié Hasegawa-Collins, 2017

Braiding Sweetgrass, by Robin Wall Kimmerer, 2013

Cattail Moonshine & Milkweed Medicine, by Tammi Hartung, 2016

Floral Emblems, by Henry Phillips, 1825

The Floral Fortune-Teller, by Sarah Mayo, 1846

Flora's Dial, by J. Wesley Hanson, circa 1846

Flora's Dictionary, by Elizabeth Gamble Wirt, 1829

Flora's Interpreter, by Sarah Hale, 1848

Flowers and Their Associations, by Anne Pratt, 1840

Flowers in Chinese Culture: Folklore, Poetry, Religion, by An Lan Zhang, 2015

Flowers of Edo: A Guide to Classical Japanese Flowers, by Kazuhiko Tajima, 2019

The Flowers Personified, by J.J. Grandville, 1847

Folklore and Symbolism of Flowers, Plants, and Trees, by Ernst Lehner and Johanna Lehner, 1960

Iwígara: American Indian Ethnobotanical Traditions and Science, by Enrique Salmón, 2020

Le Langage des Fleurs, by Charlotte de La Tour, 1819

The Language of Flowers, by Caroline M. Kirkland, 1884

The Language of Flowers: With Illustrative Poetry, edited by Frederic Shoberl, 1834

The Language of Flowers: A History, by Beverly Seaton, 1995

The Native Americans Herbal Dispensatory Handbook, by Philip Kuckunniw, 2020

The Pre-Raphaelite Language of Flowers, by Debra N. Mancoff, 2019

A Victorian Lady's Guide to Fashion and Beauty, by Mimi Matthews, 2018

The Victorian Language of Flowers, Occasional Papers from the Royal Horticultural Society Lindley Library, volume 10, edited by Dr. Brent Elliott, April 2013

Wicked Plants, by Amy Stewart, 2009

Women of Flowers, by Jack Kramer, 1996

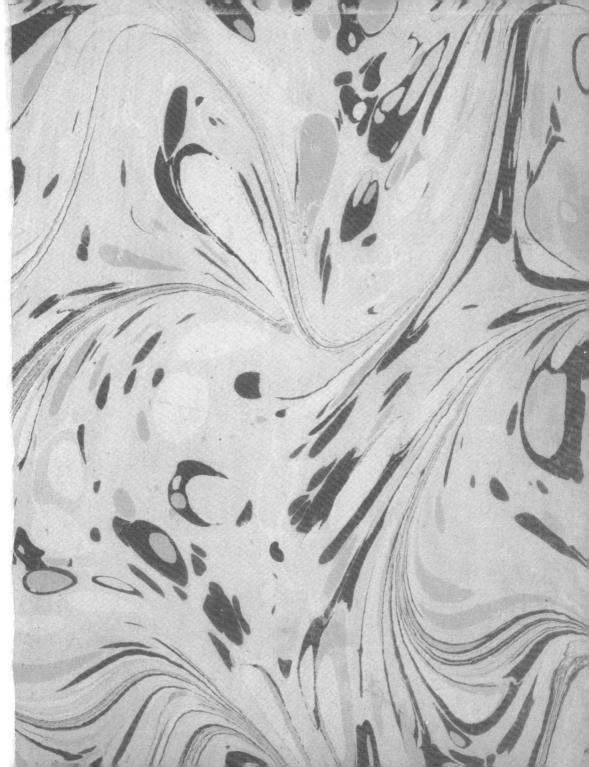